taste of home
kid APPROVED
COOKBOOK

taste of home
BOOKS

REIMAN MEDIA GROUP, LLC • GREENDALE, WI

A TASTE OF HOME/READER'S DIGEST BOOK

EDITOR-IN-CHIEF: CATHERINE CASSIDY

VICE PRESIDENT, EXECUTIVE EDITOR/BOOKS: HEIDI REUTER LLOYD

CREATIVE DIRECTOR: HOWARD GREENBERG

NORTH AMERICAN CHIEF MARKETING OFFICER: LISA KARPINSKI

FOOD DIRECTOR: DIANE WERNER, RD

SENIOR EDITOR/RETAIL BOOKS: FAITHANN STONER

EDITOR: CHRISTINE RUKAVENA

ASSOCIATE CREATIVE DIRECTOR: EDWIN ROBLES JR.

PROJECT ART DIRECTOR: JAMI ZEWEN GEITTMANN

EDITORIAL INTERN: ANDREA MESALK

CONTENT PRODUCTION MANAGER: JULIE WAGNER

LAYOUT DESIGNERS: EMMA ACEVEDO, CATHERINE FLETCHER

COPY CHIEF: DEB WARLAUMONT MULVEY

COPY EDITOR: ALYSSE GEAR

RECIPE ASSET SYSTEM MANAGER: COLEEN MARTIN

RECIPE TESTING & EDITING: TASTE OF HOME TEST KITCHEN

FOOD PHOTOGRAPHY: TASTE OF HOME PHOTO STUDIO

ADMINISTRATIVE ASSISTANT: BARB CZYSZ

The Reader's Digest Association, Inc.

PRESIDENT AND CHIEF EXECUTIVE OFFICER: TOM WILLIAMS

EXECUTIVE VICE PRESIDENT, RDA, & PRESIDENT, NORTH AMERICA: DAN LAGANI

PRESIDENT/PUBLISHER, TRADE PUBLISHING: HAROLD CLARKE

ASSOCIATE PUBLISHER: ROSANNE MCMANUS

VICE PRESIDENT, SALES & MARKETING: STACEY ASHTON

For other Taste of Home books and products, visit us at **tasteofhome.com**.

For more Reader's Digest products and information, visit **rd.com** (in the United States) or see **rd.ca** (in Canada).

INTERNATIONAL STANDARD BOOK NUMBER (10): 0-89821-911-6

INTERNATIONAL STANDARD BOOK NUMBER (13): 978-0-89821-911-1

LIBRARY OF CONGRESS CONTROL NUMBER: 2011936627

COVER PHOTOGRAPHY

Photographers: Mark Derse, Lori Foy, Rob Hagen, Dan Roberts, Grace Natoli Sheldon, James Wieland

Food Stylists: Diane Armstrong, Kaitlyn Besasie, Kathryn Conrad, Ronne Day, Sue Draheim, Alynna Malson, Leah Rekau, Shannon Roum, Sarah Thompson

Set Stylists: Sherry Bahr, Stacey Genaw, Melissa Haberman, Dee Dee Jacq, Deone Jahnke, Stephanie Marchese, Grace Natoli Sheldon, Jenna Weiler

PICTURED ON FRONT COVER (CLOCKWISE FROM TOP LEFT): Mini Burgers with the Works, page 184; Chocolate Malt Crispy Bars, page 152; Blueberry Fruit Smoothies, page 155; Kid-Sized Classic Pizza, page 107; Best Friend Cupcakes, page 179; and Blueberry Peach Muffins, page 160.

PICTURED ON BACK COVER (LEFT TO RIGHT): Peanut Butter & Jelly Waffles, page 11; Southwest Chicken, page 88; and Snowflake Tomato Soup, page 199.

PICTURED ON SPINE: Sunny Morning Doughnuts, page 10.

ADDITIONAL PHOTO CREDITS:
Mother & daughter in produce dept., page 2; Monkey Business Images/Shutterstock.com

Girls looking at book, page 206; Monkey Business Images/Shutterstock.com

Girls laughing on bed, page 209; Michelle D. Milliman/Shutterstock.com

Girls playing cards, page 210; Michelle D. Milliman/Shutterstock.com

Printed in China.
3 5 7 9 10 8 6 4

Contents

GOT A KID WHO COOKS? We're looking for kid-friendly recipes you make together, from healthy snacks to dinner and dessert. Send them to tasteofhome.com/submit.

FIND US ON FACEBOOK

FOLLOW US ON TWITTER

Build confidence and skills in the kitchen!

Cooking with your kids is fun and rewarding for everyone! You get to **enjoy quality time together,** and the entire family benefits from the delicious food you make. In fact, children are more apt to eat foods that they help cook. Everyone will feel a sense of accomplishment **the minute they taste the finished product.** Plus, your kids will learn life skills like food safety and prep, reading, fractions and teamwork in a fun, casual environment.

Getting started
Children as **young as 3** can start helping in the kitchen with simple tasks like **washing fruits or vegetables** or tearing lettuce for salads. **Older kids can peel vegetables** or **make a side dish** to go with the meal. Every job is important, because together you will make home-cooked meals.

There are many ways to **engage your children in cooking,** from choosing and reading the recipe to grocery shopping, measuring ingredients and creating the finished food.

At the market
Learning to cook doesn't have to start in the kitchen—it can start in the grocery store! When you choose a recipe, **review it together and make a shopping list of ingredients.** At the store, take time to talk about fresh produce and how to pick ripe tomatoes or a good bunch of bananas, and check out all the different sizes and shapes of pasta. Stick to your shopping list, and make healthy choices.

The grocery store is a fun and interesting place. Enjoy the sights and smells of the fresh produce by **allowing your child to pick** which apples they want or discover a new fruit or vegetable to try. Let your child order from the deli or meat counter. **Learning responsible and healthy grocery shopping is a lifelong skill.**

Kitchen safety
Kitchen safety is very important when you cook as a family. It is up to you to determine which kitchen tasks are age-appropriate for your child. No matter what age your child is, your supervision and support are important in the kitchen. Here are ways to **stay safe while having fun:**

- Wash your hands with warm soapy water before you start cooking.
- Make sure your work surfaces and utensils are clean.
- Keep sharp knives out of the reach of your child.
- Communicate with your little one when a surface is hot (stovetop, oven door, something right out of the microwave).
- Turn pot and pan handles toward the middle of the stove so no one accidentally knocks pans off.

Gadget fun
Your kitchen probably has a **variety of utensils** that will be **fascinating to young children.** Pick some age-appropriate ones and show them how they are used.

For example, practice **flipping pancakes with a spatula** and mixing things together with a whisk. See what a colander does and when it is used, and learn the **differences between a skillet and a saucepan.**

Allow yourselves extra time to talk, make mistakes, learn together and have fun!

Cooking as a team

Spending **quality time** in the kitchen **with your kids** will help them learn about food and nutrition. It may **encourage them to be more adventurous** and try new foods. Here are **kitchen tasks** your kids can do to **help you put together** a delicious, family-friendly meal:

Ages 3 to 7

- Review the recipe with you and follow along
- Wash fruits and vegetables
- Tear lettuce for salads
- Construct salads (each salad gets 4 cherry tomatoes, 6 baby carrots...)
- Mash bananas
- Retrieve ingredients for you
- Measure and mix dry ingredients
- Crack eggs (be prepared to sacrifice some!)
- Wrap potatoes in foil to bake
- Knead dough
- Smash graham crackers for crusts

Ages 8 to 12

- Roll cookie dough or meat into balls
- Set the table
- Peel vegetables
- Toast bread
- Make a sandwich
- Wash and put away dishes
- Make their school lunch (make sure it's not all cookies!)
- Unload groceries and put them away

Ages 13 & up

- Use the blender
- Use the can opener
- Press garlic
- Scramble eggs
- Cook in the microwave
- Prepare simple recipes on their own

Setting the table

A great way to **help in the kitchen** is to **set the table**. Here is what a basic table setting should look like:

1. The dinner plate is in the center of the setting and everything else is placed around it.
2. The fork goes on the left of the plate.
3. The knife goes on the right of the plate.
4. The spoon goes on the right of the knife.
5. A glass goes above the knife.
6. The napkin can be placed under the fork or on the plate.

Recipe icons

Icons have been added to recipes that may be **appropriate for your children** to help with or cook on their own. You know your children best and can judge their skill levels. **Use the icons as a general guideline.**

The **mixing bowl icon** marks recipes that **younger kids (ages 3 to 12)** will enjoy helping to prepare. They may be able to mix batter, wrap dough around hot dogs or use cookie cutters to make sandwiches in fun shapes.

The **oven mitts icon** marks recipes that **older kids (13 and older)** may prepare on their own. The recipes could involve using the microwave, stovetop or oven and may involve a small amount of chopping. Depending on their ages and abilities, your children may still need supervision.

good morning, sunshine!

strawberry-topped waffles

Taste of Home Test Kitchenn

This warm and fruity sauce takes only minutes to make. It's a nice way to present frozen waffles or even pancakes and French toast. If you don't have cranberry juice, orange juice can be used.

- 1 package (16 ounces) frozen unsweetened whole strawberries
- 1/2 cup cranberry juice, *divided*
- 2 tablespoons honey
- 2 tablespoons cornstarch
- 8 frozen waffles

1 In a large saucepan, combine the strawberries, 1/4 cup cranberry juice and honey. Cook over low heat for 10 minutes, stirring occasionally.

2 In a small bowl, combine cornstarch and remaining cranberry juice until smooth; stir into strawberry mixture. Bring to a boil; cook and stir for 2 minutes or until thickened.

3 Toast waffles according to package directions; top with warm strawberry sauce.

YIELD: 4 SERVINGS.

dad's quick bagel omelet sandwich

Andrew Nodolski, Williamstown, New Jersey

I wrap these tasty sandwiches in aluminum foil and hand them out as the kids run for the school bus!

- 1/4 cup finely chopped onion
- 1 tablespoon butter
- 4 eggs
- 1/4 cup chopped tomato
- 1/8 teaspoon salt
- 1/8 teaspoon hot pepper sauce
- 4 slices Canadian bacon
- 4 plain bagels, split
- 4 slices process American cheese

1 In a large skillet, saute onion in butter until tender. Whisk the eggs, tomato, salt and pepper sauce. Add egg mixture to skillet (mixture should set immediately at edges).

2 As eggs set, push cooked edges toward the center, letting uncooked portion flow underneath. Cook until eggs are set. Meanwhile, heat bacon in the microwave and toast bagels if desired.

3 Layer bagel bottoms with cheese. Cut omelet into fourths and serve on bagels with bacon.

YIELD: 4 SERVINGS.

glazed apple and sausage with pancakes

Cheryl Reisen, Ashland, Nebraska

This breakfast treat makes for a great kid-friendly meal. Kids don't like onions? Simply leave them out. And since most of it is made in the microwave, clean-up is a breeze.

- 2 packages (7 ounces *each*) brown-and-serve sausage links
- 1 teaspoon all-purpose flour
- 3 tablespoons water
- 1 large apple, peeled and sliced
- 1/2 cup chopped onion
- 3 tablespoons brown sugar
- 8 pancakes *or* frozen waffles, warmed

1 Heat sausage according to package directions. Meanwhile, in a 1-1/2-qt. microwave-safe dish, combine flour and water. Add apple and onion. Cover and microwave on high for 3 minutes.

2 Stir in brown sugar. Cover and cook on high for 1-2 minutes or until sugar is dissolved. Cut sausage into bite-size pieces. Add to apple mixture. Serve with pancakes.

YIELD: 4 SERVINGS.

EDITOR'S NOTE: This recipe was tested in a 1,100-watt microwave.

scrambled egg wraps

Jane Shapton, Irvine, California

This tasty morning meal, which also makes a fast dinner, will fill your family up with protein and veggies. Try using flavored wraps to jazz things up.

- 1 medium sweet red pepper, chopped
- 1 medium green pepper, chopped
- 2 teaspoons canola oil
- 5 plum tomatoes, seeded and chopped
- 6 eggs
- 1/2 cup soy milk
- 1/4 teaspoon salt
- 6 flour tortillas (8 inches), warmed

1 In a large nonstick skillet, saute peppers in oil until tender. Add tomatoes; saute 1-2 minutes longer.

2 Meanwhile, in a large bowl, whisk the eggs, soy milk and salt. Reduce heat to medium; add egg mixture to skillet. Cook and stir until eggs are completely set. Spoon 2/3 cup mixture down the center of each tortilla; roll up.

YIELD: 6 SERVINGS.

butter pecan french toast

Cathy Hall, Phoenix, Arizona

Flavored coffee creamer is the secret ingredient in this easy breakfast treat the whole family will go for. I sometimes substitute French vanilla or caramel creamer and add a little nutmeg and cinnamon to the eggs.

- 1 teaspoon plus 1 tablespoon butter, *divided*
- 1/2 cup chopped pecans
- 2 eggs
- 1/2 cup refrigerated Southern butter pecan nondairy creamer
- 6 slices French bread (1 inch thick)
- 1/4 cup confectioners' sugar
- 1/4 teaspoon ground cinnamon
Maple syrup, optional

1 In a small skillet, melt 1 teaspoon butter over medium heat. Add pecans; cook and stir for 3 minutes or until toasted. Set aside.

2 In a shallow bowl, whisk eggs and creamer. Dip bread slices in egg mixture.

3 In a large skillet, melt remaining butter over medium heat. Cook bread for 2-3 minutes on each side or until golden brown. Sprinkle with pecans, confectioners' sugar and cinnamon. Serve with maple syrup if desired.

YIELD: 3 SERVINGS.

classic potato pancakes

Arleen Osvatic, Waukesha, Wisconsin

Pass these potato pancakes around your table and compliments will follow. I serve the creamy, golden-brown pleasers with apple sauce.

2	tablespoons all-purpose flour
1	egg
1/4	cup milk
1	teaspoon salt
1/8	teaspoon pepper
2	cups grated peeled potatoes
1	tablespoon finely chopped onion
2	to 4 tablespoons canola oil

Applesauce

1 In a large bowl, whisk the flour, egg, milk, salt and pepper. Pat potatoes dry; stir into egg mixture. Add onion.

2 In a skillet, heat 2 tablespoons oil over medium heat. Pour batter by 1/4 cupfuls into skillet; cook for 2-3 minutes on each side or until golden brown, adding more oil as needed. Serve with applesauce..

YIELD: 6 PANCAKES.

sunny morning doughnuts

Sherry Flaquel, Cutler Bay, Florida

I love, love, love doughnuts, but buying them can get expensive. This recipe is economical and so delicious. It beats any store-bought doughnut.

4-1/2 to 5 cups all-purpose flour
1-1/4 cups sugar
  4 teaspoons baking powder
  1 teaspoon salt
  3 eggs, lightly beaten
  1 cup 2% milk
1/4 cup canola oil
  2 tablespoons orange juice
  4 teaspoons grated orange peel
Oil for deep-fat frying
Confectioners' sugar

1 In a large bowl, combine 4-1/2 cups flour, sugar, baking powder and salt. Combine the eggs, milk, oil, orange juice and peel; stir into dry ingredients just until moistened. Stir in enough remaining flour to form a soft dough. Cover and refrigerate for at least 1 hour.

2 Turn onto a floured surface; roll to 1/2-in. thickness. Cut with a floured 2-1/2-in. doughnut cutter.

3 In an electric skillet or deep-fat fryer, heat oil to 375°. Fry doughnuts, a few at a time, until golden brown on both sides. Drain on paper towels. Dust warm doughnuts with confectioners' sugar.

YIELD: 20 DOUGHNUTS.

peanut butter & jelly waffles

Helena Georgette Mann, Sacramento, California

Don't count out the grown-ups when it comes to craving these golden brown waffles flavored with peanut butter and just a sprinkling of cinnamon. These are guaranteed crowd-pleasers!

1-1/4 cups all-purpose flour
3 tablespoons sugar
1 tablespoon baking powder
1/4 teaspoon baking soda
1/4 teaspoon ground cinnamon
2 eggs, *separated*
1-1/4 cups milk
1/3 cup peanut butter
3 tablespoons butter, melted
Jelly of your choice

1 In a large bowl, combine the flour, sugar, baking powder, baking soda and cinnamon. In another bowl, whisk the egg yolks, milk, peanut butter and butter; stir mixture into dry ingredients just until moistened.

2 In a small bowl, beat egg whites until stiff peaks form; fold into batter. Bake in a preheated waffle iron according to manufacturer's directions until golden brown. Serve with jelly.

YIELD: 10 WAFFLES.

apple fritters

Katie Beechy, Seymour, Missouri

My kids love these fritters year-round, but I get even more requests in the fall when there are plenty of apples in season. I like to serve them as a special breakfast treat when they host friends for sleepovers.

2-1/2 cups all-purpose flour
1/2 cup nonfat dry milk powder
1/3 cup sugar
2 teaspoons baking powder
1 teaspoon salt
2 eggs
1 cup water
2 cups chopped peeled apples
Oil for deep-fat frying
Sugar

1 In a large bowl, combine first five ingredients. Whisk eggs and water; add to dry ingredients just until moistened. Fold in apples.

2 In an electric skillet, heat oil to 375°. Drop batter by teaspoonfuls, a few at a time, into hot oil. Fry until golden brown, about 1-1/2 minutes on each side. Drain on paper towels.

3 Roll warm fritters in sugar. Serve warm.

YIELD: 40 FRITTERS.

2 Turn onto a lightly floured surface; knead until smooth and elastic, about 6-8 minutes. Place in a greased bowl, turning once to grease top. Cover and let rise in a warm place until doubled, about 1 hour.

3 Turn onto a lightly floured surface; divide in half. Roll each portion into a 12-in. x 10-in. rectangle; brush with melted butter. Combine the sugar, cinnamon, chocolate chips and nuts if desired; sprinkle over each rectangle to within 1/2 in. of edges.

4 Roll up each jelly-roll style, starting with a long side; pinch seams to seal. Cut each into 10 slices. Place cut side down in a greased 15-in. x 10-in. x 1-in. baking pan. Cover and let rise until doubled, about 45 minutes.

5 Bake at 375° for 25-30 minutes or until lightly browned. Meanwhile, in a small bowl, combine the confectioners' sugar, vanilla and enough milk to reach desired consistency. Spread over rolls while slightly warm; sprinkle with additional chocolate chips if desired.

YIELD: 20 ROLLS.

chocolate cinnamon rolls

Myrna Sippel, Thompson, Illinois

With the addition of chocolate, these rolls are different from the regular cinnamon rolls. When I take them to my morning bowling league, they are quickly scarfed up.

  2 packages (1/4 ounce *each*) active dry yeast
1-1/2 cups warm water (110° to 115°), *divided*
1/2 cup butter, softened
1/2 cup sugar
  1 teaspoon salt
4-1/2 to 4-3/4 cups all-purpose flour
2/3 cup baking cocoa
FILLING:
  2 tablespoons butter, melted
1/3 cup sugar
1/2 teaspoon ground cinnamon
  1 cup miniature semisweet chocolate chips
2/3 cup finely chopped nuts, optional
ICING:
  2 cups confectioners' sugar
1/2 teaspoon vanilla extract
  2 to 3 tablespoons milk
Additional miniature semisweet chocolate chips, optional

1 In a large bowl, dissolve yeast in 1/2 cup warm water. Add the butter, sugar, salt and remaining water. Stir in 2-1/2 cups flour and cocoa. Beat on medium speed for 3 minutes or until smooth. Stir in enough remaining flour to form a soft dough.

golden cinnamon granola

Marilyn Dick, Centralia, Missouri

This basic granola with a great cinnamon flavor is perfect for a quick and hearty breakfast or snack.

1/4 cup butter, melted
1/4 cup honey
1-1/2 teaspoons ground cinnamon
1/2 teaspoon salt
  3 cups old-fashioned oats
  1 cup flaked coconut
  1 cup chopped walnuts
2/3 cup raisins

1 In a bowl, stir the butter, honey, cinnamon and salt until well blended. Combine the oats, coconut and walnuts in a greased 13-in. x 9-in. baking pan. Drizzle with butter mixture; stir to coat evenly.

2 Bake at 275° for 50-60 minutes or until golden brown, stirring every 15 minutes. Add raisins. Cool, stirring occasionally. Store in an airtight container.

YIELD: ABOUT 7 CUPS.

3 Using a metal spatula, press mixture into an ungreased 15-in. x 10-in. x 1-in. baking pan. Cool to room temperature. Cut into bars.

YIELD: 2-1/2 DOZEN.

peanut butter and jelly french toast

Flo Burtnett, Gage, Oklahoma

I've always tried to make cooking fun—for myself, my daughters and my grandchildren. Cooking teaches children the importance of following directions and being organized. This recipe is easy and kids really like it.

12	slices bread
3/4	cup peanut butter
6	tablespoons jelly *or* jam
3	eggs
3/4	cup milk
1/4	teaspoon salt
2	tablespoons butter

1 Spread peanut butter on six slices bread; spread jelly on remaining. Put a slice of each together to form sandwiches. In a large bowl, whisk eggs, milk and salt. Dip sandwiches in mixture.

2 In a large skillet, melt butter over medium heat. Cook sandwiches for 2-3 minutes on each side or until golden brown.

YIELD: 6 SERVINGS.

sunflower-cherry granola bars

Laura McDowell, Lake Villa, Illinois

These chewy bars have plenty of oats and nuts, and the dried cherries add just the right amount of tang.

4	cups old-fashioned oats
1	cup sliced almonds
1	cup flaked coconut
1	cup sugar
1	cup light corn syrup
1	cup creamy peanut butter
1/2	cup raisins
1/2	cup dried cherries
1/2	cup sunflower kernels

1 Spread oats into an ungreased 15-in. x 10-in. x 1-in. baking pan. Bake at 400° for 15-20 minutes or until lightly browned. Meanwhile, spread almonds and coconut into another ungreased 15-in. x 10-in. x 1-in. baking pan. Bake for 8-10 minutes or until lightly toasted.

2 In a Dutch oven over medium heat, bring sugar and corn syrup to a boil. Cook and stir for 2-3 minutes or until sugar is dissolved. Remove from the heat; stir in peanut butter until combined. Add the raisins, cherries, sunflower kernels, and toasted oats, almonds and coconut.

baked oatmeal

Arlene Riehl, Dundee, New York

You may think you're biting into a warm-from-the-oven oatmeal cookie when you taste this breakfast treat. It's wonderful served with milk.

- 3 cups quick-cooking oats
- 1 cup packed brown sugar
- 2 teaspoons baking powder
- 1 teaspoon salt
- 1 teaspoon ground cinnamon
- 2 eggs
- 1 cup milk
- 1/2 cup butter, melted

Additional milk

1. In a large bowl, combine the first five ingredients. In another bowl, whisk the eggs, milk and butter. Stir into oat mixture until blended.

2. Spoon into a greased 9-in. square baking pan. Bake at 350° for 40-45 minutes or until set. Serve warm with milk.

YIELD: 9 SERVINGS.

vanilla fruit salad

Nancy Dodson, Springfield, Illinois

Peach pie filling is the secret ingredient in this crowd-pleasing salad. Make it throughout the year using whatever fruits are in season.

1   pound fresh strawberries, quartered
1-1/2 cups seedless red *and/or* green grapes, halved

2   medium bananas, sliced
2   kiwifruit, peeled, sliced and quartered
1   cup cubed fresh pineapple
1   can (21 ounces) peach pie filling
3   teaspoons vanilla extract

1 In a large bowl, combine the strawberries, grapes, bananas, kiwi and pineapple. Fold in pie filling and vanilla. Chill until serving.

YIELD: 10 SERVINGS.

bird's nest breakfast cups

Aris Gonzalez, Deltona, Florida

This is a lightened-up version of an original recipe that called for regular bacon and eggs. Everyone loves it and thinks I really fussed, but it's so easy!

12   turkey bacon strips
1-1/2 cups egg substitute
6   tablespoons shredded reduced-fat Mexican cheese blend
1   tablespoon minced fresh parsley

1 In a large skillet, cook bacon over medium heat for 2 minutes on each side or until partially set but not crisp. Coat six muffin cups with cooking spray; wrap two bacon strips around the inside of each cup. Fill each with 1/4 cup egg substitute; top with cheese.

2 Bake at 350° for 18-20 minutes or until set. Cool for 5 minutes before removing from pan. Sprinkle with parsley.

YIELD: 6 SERVINGS.

pumpkin pancakes

Nancy Horsburgh, Everett, Ontario

For the perfect fall breakfast, these pancakes fit the bill. The pumpkin and cinnamon are a match made in heaven.

1   cup all-purpose flour
1   cup quick-cooking oats
2   tablespoons toasted wheat germ
2   teaspoons sugar
2   teaspoons baking powder
1/2 teaspoon salt
Pinch ground cinnamon
1   cup milk
1   egg, lightly beaten
3/4 cup canned pumpkin
2   tablespoons canola oil
Chocolate chips *or* raisins, optional

1 In a large bowl, combine the flour, oats, wheat germ, sugar, baking powder, salt and cinnamon. In a small bowl, combine the milk, egg, pumpkin and oil; stir into dry ingredients just moistened.

2 Pour batter by 1/4 cupfuls onto a hot greased griddle; turn when bubbles form on top. Cook until second side is golden brown. Decorate with chocolate chips and raisins if desired.

YIELD: 10-12 PANCAKES.

berry splash smoothies

Beth Ask, Cogan Station, Pennsylvania

These fruity smoothies are loaded with calcium and antioxidants, and they taste great on a hot day. They're pretty topped with blueberries and vanilla yogurt, but skip that step if you prefer.

- 1/4 cup fat-free milk
- 1 cup (8 ounces) cherry yogurt
- 2 cups frozen unsweetened mixed berries
- 1/4 cup fresh blueberries, *divided*
- Sugar, optional
- 3 tablespoons vanilla yogurt

1 In a blender, combine the milk, cherry yogurt, mixed berries, half of the blueberries and sugar if desired; cover and process until smooth. Stir if necessary. Pour into chilled glasses. Spoon the vanilla yogurt over the top; sprinkle with the remaining blueberries.

YIELD: 3 SERVINGS.

breakfast biscuits 'n' eggs

Teresa Huff, Nevada, Missouri

I can fix this quick breakfast using leftover biscuits or with ones baked fresh the same morning. Breakfast sandwiches are such a satisfying way to start the day, and they don't take much time at all.

- 4 individually frozen biscuits
- 2 teaspoons butter
- 4 eggs
- 4 slices process American cheese
- 4 thin slices deli ham

1 Prepare biscuits according to package directions. Meanwhile, in a large skillet, heat butter. Add eggs; reduce heat to low. Fry until the whites are completely set and yolks begin to thicken but are not hard.

2 Split the biscuits. Layer the bottom of each biscuit with cheese, ham and an egg; replace top. Microwave, uncovered, for 30-45 seconds or until cheese is melted.

YIELD: 4 BISCUITS.

EDITOR'S NOTE: This recipe was tested in a 1,100-watt microwave.

banana pancake snowmen

Phyllis Schmalz, Kansas City, Kansas

Both children and adults will love these yummy pancakes shaped like snowmen. Let little ones help decorate their characters with pretzels for arms and chocolate chips, raisins or cranberries for faces and buttons.

  1 cup complete buttermilk pancake mix
3/4 cup water
1/3 cup mashed ripe banana
  1 teaspoon confectioners' sugar
Pretzel sticks, chocolate chips, dried cranberries *and/or* halved banana slices

1 In a small bowl, stir the pancake mix, water and banana just until moistened.

2 Pour 1/4 cup batter onto a greased hot griddle, making three circles to form a snowman. Turn when bubbles form on top. Cook until the second side is golden brown. Transfer to a serving plate. Repeat with remaining batter.

3 Sprinkle with confectioners' sugar. Decorate snowmen with pretzels, chocolate chips, cranberries and/or sliced banana if desired.

YIELD: 7 SNOWMEN.

deluxe breakfast pizza

Kathy Evanko, Blairsville, Pennsylvania

I have been making this pizza for breakfast for years, and everyone who has tried it loves it. It's filling, so it keeps my gang going all morning long.

- 1 package (1/4 ounce) active dry yeast
- 1 cup warm water (110° to 115°)
- 1 tablespoon sugar
- 1 teaspoon salt
- 2-1/2 to 3 cups all-purpose flour
- 1/2 pound thinly sliced deli ham, chopped
- 1/2 pound sliced American cheese
- 1/2 pound bulk pork sausage, cooked and drained
- 2 eggs
- 3 tablespoons milk
- 2-1/2 cups (10 ounces) shredded part-skim mozzarella cheese

1 In a large bowl, dissolve yeast in warm water. Add the sugar, salt and enough flour to form a soft dough.

2 Turn onto a floured surface; knead until smooth and elastic, about 6-8 minutes. Place in a greased bowl, turning once to grease top. Cover and let rise in a warm place until doubled, about 45 minutes.

3 Punch the dough down. Press onto a lightly greased 14-in. pizza pan. Build up edges slightly. Bake at 350° for 10-12 minutes or until crust is very lightly browned.

4 Sprinkle the ham, American cheese and sausage over crust. Whisk eggs and milk; pour over toppings. Sprinkle with mozzarella. Bake for 20-25 minutes or until crust is golden and cheese is melted.

YIELD: 8 SERVINGS.

eggs in muffin cups

Lisa Walder, Urbana, Illinois

My mother used to make these all the time for our family, and now I carry on the tradition with my own. The eggs are quick to put together, and I go get ready for the day while they're in the oven. My children loved them even when they were toddlers.

- 12 thin slices deli roast beef
- 6 slices process American cheese, quartered
- 12 eggs

1 Press one slice of beef onto the bottom and up the sides of each greased muffin cup, forming a shell. Arrange two cheese pieces in each shell. Break one egg into each cup.

2 Bake, uncovered, at 350° for 20-25 minutes or until eggs are completely set.

YIELD: 6 SERVINGS (2 EACH).

french toast sticks

Taste of Home Test Kitchen

This kid-friendly classic is a handy recipe to have in your back-to-school rotation. Keep the sticks in the freezer for a hearty breakfast in an instant.

- 6 slices day-old Texas toast
- 4 eggs
- 1 cup milk
- 2 tablespoons sugar
- 1 teaspoon vanilla extract
- 1/4 to 1/2 teaspoon ground cinnamon
- 1 cup crushed cornflakes, optional
Confectioners' sugar, optional
Maple syrup

1 Cut each piece of bread into thirds; place in an ungreased 13-in. x 9-in. dish. In a large bowl, whisk the eggs, milk, sugar, vanilla and cinnamon. Pour over bread; soak for 2 minutes, turning once. Coat bread with cornflake crumbs on all sides if desired.

2 Place in a greased 15-in. x 10-in. x 1-in. baking pan. Freeze until firm, about 45 minutes. Transfer to an airtight container or resealable freezer bag and store in the freezer.

TO USE FROZEN FRENCH TOAST STICKS: Place desired number on a greased baking sheet. Bake at 425° for 8 minutes. Turn; bake 10-12 minutes longer or until golden brown. Sprinkle with confectioners' sugar if desired. Serve with syrup.

YIELD: 1-1/2 DOZEN.

3 Cover and freeze one casserole for up to 3 months. Bake remaining casserole, uncovered, at 350° for 30-35 minutes or until a knife inserted near the center comes out clean. Let stand for 10 minutes before cutting.

TO USE FROZEN CASSEROLE: Remove from the freezer 30 minutes before baking (do not thaw). Cover and bake at 350° for 55 minutes. Uncover; bake 15-20 minutes longer or until a knife inserted near the center comes out clean. Let stand for 10 minutes before cutting.

YIELD: 2 CASSEROLES (12 SERVINGS EACH).

breakfast burritos

Linda Wells, St. Mary's, Georgia

Burritos for breakfast? Why not! These zesty little handfuls will wake up your taste buds and start your day with a smile. You can make and freeze them ahead, then just pop them into the microwave for a quick meal.

  1   pound bulk pork sausage
1-1/2 cups frozen cubed hash brown potatoes
1/4   cup diced onion
1/4   cup diced green *or* red pepper
  4   eggs, lightly beaten
 12   flour tortillas (8 inches), warmed
1/2   cup shredded cheddar cheese
Picante sauce and sour cream, optional

1 In a large skillet, cook sausage over medium heat until no longer pink; drain. Add the potatoes, onion and pepper; cook and stir for 6-8 minutes or until tender. Add eggs; cook and stir until set.

2 Spoon filling off center on each tortilla. Sprinkle with cheese. Fold sides and ends over filling and roll up. Serve with picante sauce and sour cream if desired.

TO FREEZE AND REHEAT BURRITOS: Wrap each burrito in waxed paper and foil. Freeze for up to 1 month. To use, remove foil and waxed paper. Place one burrito on a microwave-safe plate. Microwave on high for 2 to 2-1/4 minutes or until a meat thermometer reads 165°, turning burrito over once. Let stand for 20 seconds.

YIELD: 12 BURRITOS.

EDITOR'S NOTE: This recipe was tested in a 1,100-watt microwave.

ham and egg breakfast casseroles

Lisa Pogue, Keithville, Louisiana

I made this for my family one day as I tried using things up in my fridge. Even my picky children loved it!

  1   pound fresh mushrooms, coarsely chopped
1/3   cup butter, cubed
1/2   teaspoon Italian seasoning
1/8   teaspoon pepper
  4   cups (16 ounces) shredded sharp cheddar cheese
1-3/4 cups cubed fully cooked ham
1/2   cup shredded Parmesan cheese
  2   tablespoons all-purpose flour
 24   eggs
  2   cups heavy whipping cream
  1   tablespoon Dijon mustard
1/8   teaspoon white pepper

1 In a Dutch oven, saute mushrooms in butter until tender. Add Italian seasoning and pepper; saute 1 minute longer. Spread mushroom mixture evenly into two greased 13-in. x 9-in. baking dishes.

2 In a large bowl, combine the cheddar cheese, ham, Parmesan cheese and flour. Sprinkle over the mushroom mixture. Whisk the eggs, cream, mustard and white pepper; pour egg mixture into baking dishes.

puff pancake with blueberry sauce

Barbara Mohr, Millington, Michigan

I collect cookbooks and discovered this recipe while I was in Texas on vacation. The light and puffy pancake really does melt in your mouth! It's a definite family-pleaser.

- 2 tablespoons butter
- 2 eggs
- 1/2 cup milk
- 1/2 cup all-purpose flour
- 2 tablespoons sugar
- 1/8 teaspoon ground cinnamon

BLUEBERRY SAUCE:

- 1/4 cup packed brown sugar
- 1 tablespoon cornstarch
- 1/4 cup orange juice
- 1 cup fresh *or* frozen blueberries
- 1/4 teaspoon vanilla extract

1 Place butter in a 9-in. pie plate; place in a 425° oven for 4-5 minutes or until melted. Meanwhile, in a small bowl, whisk eggs and milk. In another small bowl, combine the flour, sugar and cinnamon; whisk in egg mixture until smooth. Pour into prepared pie plate. Bake for 18-22 minutes or until sides are crisp and golden brown.

2 Meanwhile, in a small saucepan, combine brown sugar and cornstarch. Gradually whisk in orange juice until smooth. Stir in blueberries. Bring to a boil over medium heat, stirring constantly. Cook and stir 1-2 minutes longer or until thickened. Remove from the heat; stir in vanilla. Serve with pancake.

YIELD: 4 SERVINGS.

breakfast quesadillas

Jennifer Evans, Oceanside, California

Fluffy eggs and crispy tortillas make this speedy recipe great for breakfast or brunch. The mild cheese, onions and bacon offer the perfect mix of flavors. Serve these yummy quesadillas with your favorite condiments.

    3   eggs
    2   flour tortillas (8 inches)
  1/2   cup shredded fontina cheese
    2   bacon strips, cooked and crumbled
    1   green onion, thinly sliced
Sour cream and salsa, optional

1   In a small bowl, whisk the eggs. Coat a large skillet with cooking spray. Add eggs; cook and stir over medium heat until completely set.

2   Place tortillas on a griddle. Spoon eggs over half of each tortilla; sprinkle with cheese, bacon and onion. Fold over and cook over low heat for 1-2 minutes on each side or until cheese is melted. Serve with sour cream and salsa.

YIELD: 2 SERVINGS.

cheddar-ham oven omelet

Betty Abrey, Imperial, Saskatchewan

We had a family reunion for 50 relatives from the U.S. and Canada, and it took four pans of this hearty, five-ingredient omelet to feed the crowd. Fresh fruit and an assortment of muffins helped round out our brunch menu.

16 eggs
2 cups milk
2 cups (8 ounces) shredded cheddar cheese
3/4 cup cubed fully cooked ham
6 green onions, chopped

1 In a large bowl, whisk eggs and milk. Stir in the cheese, ham and onions. Pour into a greased 13-in. x 9-in. baking dish.

2 Bake, uncovered, at 350° for 40-45 minutes or until a knife inserted near the center comes out clean. Let stand for 10 minutes before cutting.

YIELD: 12 SERVINGS.

blueberry pancakes

Annemarie Pietila, Farmington Hills, Michigan

These light, fluffy pancakes are made in a little batch, so there's no need to worry about what to do with leftover batter. For a special treat, I like to prepare them with delicious blueberries.

1-1/4 cups all-purpose flour
1 tablespoon sugar
1 teaspoon baking powder
1/2 teaspoon baking soda
1/2 teaspoon salt
1 egg, beaten
1-1/4 cups buttermilk
2 tablespoons canola oil
1 cup fresh *or* frozen blueberries, optional

1 In a large bowl, combine the flour, sugar, baking powder, baking soda and salt. Combine the egg, buttermilk and oil; stir into dry ingredients just until blended. Fold in blueberries if desired.

2 Pour batter by 1/4 cupfuls onto a lightly greased hot griddle; turn when bubbles form on top of pancakes. Cook until second side is golden brown.

YIELD: ABOUT 8 PANCAKES.

EDITOR'S NOTE: For dollar-size pancakes, drop batter by tablespoonfuls onto a griddle.

ham 'n' egg submarine

DeeDee Newton, Toronto, Ontario

Whenever the whole family gets together for a holiday or long weekend, they request this big breakfast sandwich. I can feed everyone by stacking our favorite breakfast fixings inside a loaf of French bread.

- 1 unsliced loaf (1 pound) French bread
- 4 tablespoons butter, softened, *divided*
- 2 tablespoons mayonnaise
- 8 thin slices deli ham
- 1 large tomato, sliced
- 1 small onion, thinly sliced
- 8 eggs, lightly beaten
- 8 slices cheddar cheese

1 Cut bread in half lengthwise; carefully hollow out top and bottom, leaving 1/2-in. shells (discard removed bread or save for another use). Spread 3 tablespoons of butter and all of the mayonnaise inside bread shells. Line bottom bread shell with ham; top with tomato and onion.

2 In a large skillet, melt remaining butter; add eggs. Cook over medium heat, stirring occasionally until edges are almost set.

3 Spoon into bottom bread shell; top with cheese. Cover with bread top. Wrap in greased foil. Bake at 375° for 15-20 minutes or until heated through. Cut into serving-size pieces.

YIELD: 6-8 SERVINGS.

wagon wheel breakfast pie

Sandra Hough, Hampton, Virginia

This cute eye-opener is loaded with flavor. The recipe originally came from a military magazine. I've prepared it several times and it's quite popular—especially with kids.

1-1/2 cups frozen shredded hash brown
      potatoes, thawed
- 3 tablespoons cream cheese, softened
- 2 tablespoons plus 2 teaspoons 2% milk, *divided*
- 1 green onion, chopped
- 1/8 teaspoon salt, optional
Dash pepper
- 4 uncooked breakfast sausage links
- 1/4 cup biscuit/baking mix
- 1 egg
Dash ground nutmeg
Dash paprika

1 Place the hash browns in a 7-in. pie plate coated with cooking spray. In a small bowl, combine the cream cheese, 2 tablespoons milk, onion, salt if desired and pepper; spread over potatoes.

2 Cut sausage links in half lengthwise; arrange over potatoes in a spoke-like fashion.

3 In a small bowl, whisk the biscuit mix, egg, nutmeg and remaining milk until smooth; pour between sausages. Sprinkle with paprika.

4 Bake at 400° for 25-30 minutes or until golden brown and filling is bubbly.

YIELD: 2 SERVINGS.

blueberry banana smoothies

Lisa DeMarsh, Mt. Solon, Virginia

We often make smoothies to use up bananas that are past the point of eating them fresh. This combination is a favorite.

- 1   medium ripe banana, cut into chunks
- 1   cup frozen unsweetened blueberries
- 1   cup cherry juice blend
- 3/4   cup vanilla yogurt
- 1/2   cup crushed ice
- Dash ground cinnamon

1   In a blender, combine all ingredients; cover and process for 30 seconds or until smooth. Pour into chilled glasses; serve immediately.

YIELD: 3 SERVINGS.

banana chip pancakes

Christeen Przepioski, Newark, California

Perfect for weekends or a special birthday-morning treat, these fluffy pancakes can be customized to your heart's content! One of my kids eats the plain banana pancakes, another likes just chocolate chips added, and a third one goes for the works.

2 cups biscuit/baking mix
1 egg
1 cup milk
1 cup mashed ripe bananas
3/4 cup swirled milk chocolate and peanut butter chips
Maple syrup and additional swirled milk chocolate and peanut butter chips, optional

1 Place biscuit mix in a large bowl. Combine the egg, milk and bananas; stir into biscuit mix just until moistened. Stir in chips.

2 Pour batter by 1/4 cupfuls onto a greased hot griddle; turn when bubbles form on top. Cook until the second side is golden brown. Serve with syrup and additional chips if desired.

YIELD: 12 PANCAKES.

hearty egg scramble

Marsha Ransom, South Haven, Michigan

Scrambled eggs with meat and potatoes for breakfast is always a satisfying choice. Switch up the veggies to your family's liking.

- 1/3 cup chopped onion
- 1/4 cup chopped green pepper
- 1/4 cup butter
- 2 medium potatoes, peeled, cooked and cubed
- 1-1/2 cups julienned fully cooked ham
- 6 eggs
- 2 tablespoons water
- Dash pepper

1 In a large skillet, saute onion and green pepper in butter until crisp-tender. Add potatoes and ham; cook and stir for 5 minutes.

2 In a large bowl, whisk the eggs, water and pepper; pour over ham mixture. Cook and stir over medium heat until eggs are completely set.

YIELD: 6 SERVINGS.

berry ba-nanza smoothies

Brenda Strohm, Omaha, Nebraska

I keep several bananas in the freezer so I'm always ready to whip up this thick beverage for a quick breakfast or a tasty treat. Frozen fruit gives it a great consistency—it's like drinking a berry milk shake!

- 1 cup vanilla yogurt
- 1 medium ripe banana, peeled, cut into chunks and frozen
- 1/4 cup *each* frozen unsweetened strawberries, blueberries, raspberries and blackberries
- 1 cup fat-free milk

1 In a blender, combine all the ingredients; cover and process until smooth. Pour into chilled glasses; serve immediately.

YIELD: 3 SERVINGS.

pumpkin pie oatmeal

Amber Rife, Columbus, Ohio

I made this oatmeal because I love pumpkin pie and wanted it for breakfast. It's so smooth and creamy.

- 1 cup water
- 1 cup vanilla soy milk
- 1 cup old-fashioned oats
- 1/2 cup canned pumpkin
- 1/4 teaspoon pumpkin pie spice
- 2 tablespoons sugar
- 1/4 teaspoon vanilla extract

Dried cranberries, optional

1 In a small saucepan, combine the water, soy milk, oats, pumpkin and pie spice. Bring to a boil; cook and stir for 5 minutes.

2 Remove from the heat; stir in sugar and vanilla. Sprinkle with cranberries if desired.

YIELD: 2 SERVINGS.

maple sausage patties

Margaret Eid, Huron, South Dakota

Maple syrup, sage and thyme give delightful flavor to these homemade breakfast patties.

- 1 pound ground pork
- 1 tablespoon maple syrup
- 1/2 teaspoon salt
- 1/2 teaspoon onion powder
- 1/2 teaspoon rubbed sage
- 1/2 teaspoon dried thyme
- 1/2 teaspoon poultry seasoning
- 1/2 teaspoon ground nutmeg
- 1/4 teaspoon cayenne pepper
- 1 to 2 teaspoons mesquite Liquid Smoke, optional

1 In a large bowl, combine all of the ingredients. Shape into eight 2-1/2-in. patties. Cover and refrigerate for at least 1 hour.

2 In a large nonstick skillet coated with cooking spray, cook patties over medium heat for 4-6 minutes on each side or until meat is no longer pink and a meat thermometer reads 160°.

YIELD: 8 SERVINGS.

build a better oatmeal!

Children will love creating their own culinary delights with these stir-in ideas:

- Dried fruits like raisins, cherries or currants
- Nuts and berries
- Fresh apples or applesauce
- Maple syrup or honey
- Cinnamon or pie spice
- Chocolate chips or cocoa powder
- Vanilla yogurt

Also think about these:

- Pie for breakfast (oatmeal with fruity pie filling and graham crackers) could be a special-occasion treat for graduation, weekend at Grandma's, or a birthday!
- Wheat germ and ground flaxseed are nearly imperceptible in cooked oatmeal, yet they pack a powerful nutrition boost.

hash brown sausage bake

Vicky Dempsey, Louisville, Mississippi

This is one of my son's favorites. Buttery hash browns are the mouthwatering crust for a yummy filling of sausage and cheese. It's sure to please at breakfast, brunch or even lunch.

- 1 package (20 ounces) refrigerated shredded hash brown potatoes
- 1/3 cup butter, melted
- 1 teaspoon beef bouillon granules
- 1 pound bulk pork sausage
- 1/3 cup chopped onion
- 1 cup (8 ounces) 4% cottage cheese
- 3 eggs, lightly beaten
- 4 slices process American cheese, chopped

1 In a large bowl, combine the hash browns, butter and bouillon. Press onto the bottom and up the sides of a greased 10-in. pie plate. Bake at 350° for 25-30 minutes or until edges are lightly browned.

2 Meanwhile, in a large skillet, cook the sausage and onion over medium heat until the meat is no longer pink; drain. In a large bowl, combine the sausage mixture, cottage cheese, eggs and American cheese.

3 Pour into crust. Bake at 350° for 40-45 minutes or until a knife inserted near the center comes out clean. Let stand for 5 minutes before cutting.

YIELD: 6-8 SERVINGS.

breakfast pizza

Loretta Kemna, St. Elizabeth, Missouri

Topped with favorite breakfast ingredients, including eggs, sausage and hash browns, this colorful pizza makes a hearty centerpiece for a special breakfast. Its tiny size is just right for two!

- 1 tube (4 ounces) refrigerated crescent rolls
- 1/4 pound bulk pork sausage *or* 4 pork sausage links, sliced
- 1/2 cup frozen shredded hash brown potatoes, thawed
- 2 tablespoons diced sweet red pepper
- 2 tablespoons diced green pepper
- 1/2 cup shredded cheddar cheese
- 2 eggs
- 2 tablespoons 2% milk
- 1/8 teaspoon pepper
- 1 tablespoon shredded Parmesan cheese

1 Separate crescent dough into four triangles; arrange on an ungreased 7-1/2-in. round pizza pan with points toward the center. Press onto the bottom of pan, building up edges slightly.

2 In a small skillet, cook sausage over medium heat until no longer pink; drain. Sprinkle over crust. Top with potatoes, peppers and cheddar cheese.

3 In a small bowl, whisk the eggs, milk and pepper. Pour over pizza; sprinkle with cheese.

4 Bake at 375° for 20-25 minutes or until eggs are completely set and top is golden brown. Cut into slices.

YIELD: 2 SERVINGS.

baked cinnamon doughnuts

Kathi Grenier, Auburn, Maine

Baking these old-fashioned delights is a fantastic alternative to frying. Homemade doughnuts are a treat the whole family will appreciate.

- 2 packages (1/4 ounce *each*) active dry yeast
- 1/3 cup warm water (110° to 115°)
- 1-1/2 cups warm milk (110° to 115°)
- 1/3 cup shortening
- 2 eggs
- 1-1/4 cups sugar, *divided*
- 2 teaspoons ground nutmeg
- 1-1/2 teaspoons salt
- 4-1/2 to 5 cups all-purpose flour
- 1/3 cup butter, melted
- 1 teaspoon ground cinnamon

1 In a large bowl, dissolve yeast in water. Add milk and shortening; stir for 1 minute. Add eggs, 1/4 cup sugar, nutmeg, salt and 2 cups flour; beat on low speed until smooth. Stir in enough remaining flour to form a soft dough (do not knead). Cover and let rise in a warm place until doubled, about 1 hour.

2 Punch dough down. Turn onto a floured surface; roll out to 1/2-in. thickness. Cut with a 2-3/4-in. doughnut cutter; place 1 in. apart on greased baking sheets. Cover and let rise in a warm place until doubled, about 30 minutes.

3 Bake at 450° for 7-8 minutes or until lightly browned. Brush with butter. In a shallow bowl, combine cinnamon and remaining sugar; roll warm doughnuts in mixture. Serve immediately.

YIELD: ABOUT 2 DOZEN.

strawberry banana smoothies

Christy Adkins, Martinez, Georgia

Ice and frozen berries keep these frosty smoothies extra thick. Best of all, the recipe is a great way to use up that last banana.

- 1/2 cup 2% milk
- 1/3 cup strawberry yogurt
- 1/3 cup frozen unsweetened strawberries
- 1/2 medium firm banana, chopped
- 4 ice cubes
- 8 teaspoons sugar

1 In a blender, combine all of the ingredients; cover and process for 30-45 seconds or until smooth. Stir if necessary. Pour into chilled glasses; serve immediately.

YIELD: 2 SERVINGS.

cocoa pancakes

Lisa DeMarsh, Mt. Solon, Virginia

We love these chocolaty whole wheat pancakes that feel like a yummy treat. The yogurt and raspberries are a tasty and good-for-you accent. Use one egg if you don't have egg substitute on hand.

3/4 cup whole wheat flour
1/4 cup sugar
2 tablespoons baking cocoa
1 teaspoon baking powder
1/8 teaspoon salt
1/8 teaspoon ground nutmeg
3/4 cup fat-free milk
1/4 cup egg substitute
1 tablespoon reduced-fat butter, melted
1 cup fresh raspberries
1/2 cup fat-free vanilla yogurt

1 In a small bowl, combine the first six ingredients. Combine the milk, egg substitute and butter; add to dry ingredients just until moistened.

2 Pour batter by scant 1/4 cupfuls onto a hot griddle coated with cooking spray; turn when bubbles form on top. Cook until the second side is lightly browned. Serve with raspberries and yogurt.

YIELD: 8 PANCAKES.

EDITOR'S NOTE: This recipe was tested with Land O'Lakes light stick butter.

orange fruit baskets

Taste of Home Test Kitchen

Pretty baskets brimming with fruit are a fun and healthy way to start the day. Little ones will enjoy washing the fruit and helping to fill these delightful baskets.

10 large navel oranges
1 kiwifruit, peeled, sliced and quartered
3/4 cup fresh blueberries
3/4 cup sliced fresh strawberries
3/4 cup halved green grapes
3/4 cup halved red grapes
Additional red grapes and blueberries, optional

1 Peel and section two oranges; set aside. Make baskets from remaining oranges. For handle, score a 1/2-in.-wide strip over the top of each orange. Score peel from the base of the handle on one side to the opposite side. Cut along scored lines with a paring knife and remove peel. Repeat on other side.

2 Using a paring or grapefruit knife and spoon, scoop out pulp from under handle and inside of basket. Combine kiwi, blueberries, strawberries, grapes and reserved orange segments; spoon into baskets.

3 If desired, make a flower on top of basket handle with grapes and blueberries. Quarter six grapes; place three quarters on top of each handle with a blueberry in the center.

YIELD: 8 BASKETS.

breakfast casserole

Sorrel Pickle, Arcadia, Florida

This is a good breakfast dish when you're short on time. It's simple to prepare and can be made early or even frozen until needed.

- 2 slices bread
- 1/2 pound bulk pork sausage
- 1/2 cup shredded cheddar cheese
- 3 eggs
- 1 cup milk
- 1/2 teaspoon ground mustard
- 1/4 teaspoon salt
- 1/8 teaspoon pepper

1 Remove crusts from bread; cut bread into 1-in. cubes. Place in a greased 8-in. square baking dish.

2 In a small skillet, brown the sausage over medium heat until no longer pink; drain. Sprinkle the sausage and cheese over bread cubes.

3 In a small bowl, whisk the eggs, milk, mustard, salt and pepper. Pour over the sausage and cheese. Bake at 350° for 30 minutes or until puffed and golden.

YIELD: 2-4 SERVINGS.

big-batch granola

Wilma Beller, Hamilton, Ohio

This is one of my family's favorite breakfasts. It gives them the energy they need to get through the day's chores.

- 4 cups old-fashioned oats
- 1/3 cup honey *or* molasses
- 1/4 cup canola oil
- 1 teaspoon vanilla extract
- 1 cup chopped nuts
- 3/4 cup uncooked oat bran cereal
- 1 cup flaked coconut
- 1 cup raisins
- 1 cup chopped dates

Yogurt and fresh fruit, optional

1 Spread rolled oats on a 15-in. x 10-in. baking pan. Bake at 350° for 5 minutes. Stir; bake 5 minutes longer or until toasted. Meanwhile, combine honey and oil in a small saucepan. Cook and stir over medium heat for 2-3 minutes or until heated through. Remove from the heat; stir in extract. Remove oats from oven; toss with nuts, bran and coconut.

2 Pour hot honey mixture over oat mixture; toss well. Return to oven and bake 20-25 minutes, stirring every 6 minutes. Remove from oven. Stir in raisins and dates. Cool. Store in an airtight container. Serve with yogurt and fresh fruit of your choice if desired.

YIELD: 8 CUPS.

EDITOR'S NOTE: Look for oat bran cereal near the hot cereals or in the natural foods section.

egg 'n' potato burritos

Ann Baker, Texarkana, Texas

This is my husband's favorite dish. The scrumptious combination of hash browns and eggs adds zip to breakfasts on the fly.

- 1 cup frozen shredded hash brown potatoes
- 3 green onions, chopped
- 1 tablespoon olive oil
- 8 eggs, beaten
- 1 can (14-1/2 ounces) diced tomatoes with mild green chilies, drained
- 1/2 teaspoon salt
- 1/2 teaspoon pepper
- 6 fat-free flour tortillas (8 inches), warmed
- 1 cup (4 ounces) shredded reduced-fat cheddar cheese

1 In a large nonstick skillet, cook potatoes and onions in oil over medium heat for 8-10 minutes or until potatoes are tender, stirring occasionally.

2 In a large bowl, combine the eggs, tomatoes, salt and pepper. Pour over potatoes. Reduce heat to medium-low. Cook and stir until eggs are completely set. Remove from the heat.

3 Spoon about 1/2 cup of egg mixture down the center of each tortilla; sprinkle with cheese. Fold sides and ends over filling and roll up.

YIELD: 6 SERVINGS.

santa pancakes

Taste of Home Test Kitchen

For a meal sure to make little eyes shine bright, try this adorable breakfast treat. The cinnamon-flavored pancakes feature cherries and whipped cream, so they look just like the jolly ol' elf himself.

- 2 cups biscuit/baking mix
- 1 teaspoon ground cinnamon
- 2 eggs
- 1 cup milk
- 1 teaspoon vanilla extract
- 2 medium bananas, sliced
- 18 semisweet chocolate chips
- 1 can (21 ounces) cherry pie filling
   Whipped cream in a can

1 In a large bowl, combine baking mix and cinnamon. In a small bowl, whisk the eggs, milk and vanilla; stir into dry ingredients just until moistened.

2 Pour batter by 1/4 cupfuls onto a greased hot griddle. Turn when bubbles form on top; cook until second side is golden brown.

3 Place pancakes on individual plates. For Santa's eyes, place two banana slices on each pancake; top with a chocolate chip. For ears, cut remaining banana slices in half; place on either side of pancake. For nose, remove nine cherries from pie filling; place one in the center of each pancake. Spoon 1/4 cup pie filling above pancake for hat. Use whipped cream to spray the beard, hat brim and pom-pom.

YIELD: 9 SERVINGS.

lunch on the go

turkey lunch-box wraps

Denise Marshall, Jacksonville, Florida

You'll get a delicious head start on your veggies for the day with this turkey-and-much-more wrap! These sandwiches taste wonderful cold or warmed in the microwave. They make a great brown-bag treat.

- 2   whole wheat tortillas (8 inches), room temperature
- 4   teaspoons honey mustard
- 6   ounces thinly sliced deli turkey
- 2   thin slices Muenster cheese
- 1   cup fresh baby spinach
- 1   medium carrot, shredded
- 1   bacon strip, cooked and crumbled
- 1/4 cup chopped seeded cucumber
- 1/4 cup chopped roasted sweet red pepper

1 Spread tortillas with mustard. Layer each with turkey, cheese, spinach, carrot, bacon, cucumber and red pepper; roll up tightly.

YIELD: 2 SERVINGS.

chocolate fluffernutter sandwiches

Taste of Home Test Kitchen

These fun sandwiches are sure to be greeted with smiles when they're served with sliced bananas and a glass of milk for lunch.

- 1/4 cup chunky peanut butter
- 4   thick slices white bread
- 1   tablespoon chocolate syrup
- 1/4 cup marshmallow creme

1 Spread peanut butter on two slices of bread. Drizzle with chocolate syrup; spread with marshmallow creme. Top with remaining bread.

YIELD: 2 SERVINGS.

deli ranch wraps

Taste of Home Test Kitchen

Here's a cool idea that's ready to gobble up in no time. It's a terrific use for deli turkey. Just add lettuce, tomato, green pepper, shredded cheese and ranch dressing for a flavorful blend.

- 8 thin slices cooked turkey
- 4 flour tortillas (6 inches), room temperature
- 1 large tomato, thinly sliced
- 1 medium green pepper, cut into thin strips
- 1 cup shredded lettuce
- 1 cup (4 ounces) shredded cheddar cheese
- 1/3 cup ranch salad dressing

1 Place two slices of turkey on each tortilla. Layer with tomato, green pepper, lettuce and cheese. Drizzle with salad dressing. Roll up tightly.

YIELD: 4 SERVINGS.

cherry-chicken pasta salad

Tina Matro, Suttons Bay, Michigan

This sweet and savory salad always wins me compliments on my cooking. The dried cherries add a hint of pretty color and delicious burst of fruit.

- 2-1/2 cups uncooked bow tie pasta
- 3-1/2 cups shredded cooked chicken
- 3 celery ribs, chopped
- 6 green onions, chopped
- 3/4 cup dried cherries
- 1 cup mayonnaise
- 2 teaspoons sugar
- 1/2 teaspoon salt
- 1/2 teaspoon Dijon mustard
- 1/8 teaspoon pepper
- Dash dried tarragon

1 Cook pasta according to package directions. Meanwhile, in a large bowl, combine the chicken, celery, onions and cherries. Drain pasta and rinse in cold water; add to chicken mixture.

2 Combine the mayonnaise, sugar, salt, mustard, pepper and tarragon. Pour over salad and toss to coat. Chill until serving.

YIELD: 6 SERVINGS.

lunch on a stick

Sara Martin, Brookfield, Wisconsin

It's fun to create different lunch combinations with my mom. I like to make patterns.

Block of cheddar *or* Colby-Monterey Jack cheese
Cooked tortellini
Grape tomatoes
Whole wheat bread slices, cut into 1-inch pieces
Leaf lettuce, optional
Sliced deli ham, cut into 1-inch strips
Seedless red *or* green grapes
Wooden skewers (5 to 6 inches)

1 Cut cheese into 1/4-in. slices and then into 1-in. pieces. (Smaller pieces may break when threaded on the skewer.)

2 Mac & Cheese on a Stick: Alternately thread cheese and tortellini on a skewer. Add grape tomatoes if desired.

3 Ham & Cheese on a Stick: Thread bread, lettuce if desired, cheese and a ribbon of ham on a skewer. Add additional cheese and bread pieces. Hold in place with a grape or grape tomato on each end.

4 Fruit & Cheese on a Stick: Alternately thread grapes and cheese on a skewer.

5 Create your own Lunch on a Stick: Let children place their favorite ingredients on a stick.

YIELD: 4 SERVINGS.

chicken alphabet soup

Sarah Mackey, New Smyrna Beach, Florida

I'm a teenager and love to make this fun chicken soup for my family. It makes me so happy when they tell me how much they like it!

- 3 medium carrots, chopped
- 2 celery ribs, chopped
- 3/4 cup chopped sweet onion
- 1 tablespoon olive oil
- 2 quarts chicken broth
- 3 cups cubed cooked chicken breast
- 1/4 teaspoon dried thyme
- 1-1/2 cups uncooked alphabet pasta
- 3 tablespoons minced fresh parsley

1 In a Dutch oven, saute the carrots, celery and onion in oil until tender. Stir in the broth, chicken and thyme. Bring to a boil. Stir in pasta.

2 Reduce heat; simmer, uncovered, for 10 minutes or until pasta is tender. Stir in parsley.

YIELD: 10 SERVINGS (2-1/2 QUARTS).

fruit 'n' nut clusters

Alexandra Marcotty, Cleveland Heights, Ohio

Easy as 1-2-3, these fuss-free treats are ready in a snap. The flavors blend well, creating the perfect bite-sized snack that's wholesome, too!

- 1 cup vanilla *or* white chips
- 1/3 cup dried cranberries
- 1/3 cup salted whole cashews

1 In a microwave-safe bowl, melt chips; stir until smooth. Stir in the cranberries and cashews. Drop by tablespoonfuls onto a waxed paper-lined baking sheet. Refrigerate until firm. Store in an airtight container.

YIELD: 1 DOZEN.

ham 'n' swiss envelopes

Tammy Burgess, Loveland, Ohio

These clever envelopes will make people eager to look inside. The hot pockets shaped with refrigerated dough are stuffed with a delicious ham and cheese filling.

3/4   cup diced fully cooked ham
4   teaspoons finely chopped onion
1   teaspoon canola oil
3/4   cup shredded Swiss cheese
1   package (3 ounces) cream cheese, cubed
2   tubes (8 ounces *each*) refrigerated crescent rolls

1 In a large skillet, saute ham and onion in oil until onion is tender. Add cheeses; cook for 3-4 minutes or until melted. Remove from the heat; set aside.

2 Unroll crescent dough and separate into four rectangles; seal perforations. Place 2 tablespoons of ham mixture in the center of each rectangle. Starting with a short side, fold a third of the dough over filling. On the other short side, bring both corners together in the center to form a point. Fold over to resemble an envelope. Pinch seams to seal.

3 Place on an ungreased baking sheet. Bake at 400° for 10-12 minutes or until golden brown.

YIELD: 4 SERVINGS.

1 Leaving the rolls attached, cut in half horizontally; remove top. Spread ranch dressing over cut side of top; spread mustard over cut side of bottom. Layer with ham, salami and turkey; replace top. Cut into four sandwiches.

YIELD: 2 SERVINGS.

frozen fruit salad

Virginia Powell, Eureka, Kansas

I use this recipe to add a healthy twist to brown-bag lunches. I'm always in a hurry in the morning, so having a ready-made salad is a great help.

- 1 can (16 ounces) apricot halves, drained
- 1 container (16 ounces) frozen sweetened sliced strawberries, thawed and drained
- 3/4 cup pineapple tidbits
- 3 medium bananas, sliced
- 1 can (6 ounces) frozen orange juice concentrate, thawed
- 1 juice can water

1 In a food processor, chop apricots. In a bowl, combine the apricots, strawberries, pineapple, bananas, orange juice and water. Ladle into muffin cups sprayed with cooking spray. Freeze.

2 When frozen, quickly remove salads to freezer bags or tightly covered storage containers. When packing a lunch, place salad in an individual storage container in a thermal lunch bag and it will thaw by lunchtime.

YIELD: 22-24 SERVINGS.

hawaiian deli sandwiches

Tammy Blomquist, Taylorville, Illinois

When our kids were in sports, we were often on the road for meals. These easy sandwiches can be made ahead of time, and they travel well. They're great for potlucks and entertaining, too.

- 1 package (4.4 ounces) Hawaiian sweet rolls
- 1 tablespoon ranch salad dressing
- 1 tablespoon prepared mustard
- 2 slices deli ham
- 4 slices hard salami
- 2 slices deli turkey

pack a lunch they'll LOVE!

Include something from each category for a nutritious lunch your kids will love.

- Protein: peanut or almond butter, boiled eggs, tuna salad, meat or beans
- Whole grains: bread, tortillas, pitas, crackers, rice or granola
- Dairy: milk, yogurt, cottage cheese or cheese
- Fruits: mix up the colors and use 100% juice in moderation
- Vegetables: carrots, celery, snap peas and cherry tomatoes are popular. Choose something your children will enjoy, and occasionally throw in a little veggie dip for fun! And don't forget vegetable soup.

3 Wrap each burrito in paper towel, then in foil. Repeat with remaining tortillas and filling. Refrigerate. Eat burritos cold, or remove foil and heat paper towel-wrapped burrito in a microwave on high for 30-60 seconds.

YIELD: 15-20 SERVINGS.

homemade lemonade

(pictured at right)

Rebecca Baird, Salt Lake City, Utah

Who doesn't love chilled lemonade on a hot day? Made with club soda, this version is slightly bubbly and bursting with citrus flavor.

3/4 cup sugar
1/2 cup water
1/4 cup lemon peel strips (about 1-1/2 lemons)
3/4 cup lemon juice (about 3 lemons)
1 cup club soda, chilled

1 In a small saucepan, heat sugar and water over medium heat until sugar is dissolved, stirring frequently. Stir in lemon peel strips. Bring to a boil. Reduce heat; simmer, uncovered, for 5 minutes. Cool slightly.

2 Transfer to a pitcher. Stir in lemon juice; refrigerate until chilled. Discard lemon peel strips. Stir in club soda. Serve over ice.

YIELD: 2-1/2 CUPS.

brown-bag burritos

Rhonda Cliett, Belton, Texas

Not many people consider burritos in a brown-bag lunch, but we really enjoy them. They're tasty cold and easy to heat if a microwave's available.

1 pound ground beef
1 can (16 ounces) refried beans
2/3 cup enchilada sauce
1/4 cup water
3 tablespoons finely chopped onion
4-1/2 teaspoons chili powder
1-1/2 teaspoons garlic powder
3/4 teaspoon salt
1/2 teaspoon dried oregano
15 to 20 flour tortillas (8 inches)
1-1/2 to 2-1/2 cups shredded cheddar cheese

1 In a large skillet, cook beef until no longer pink; drain. Stir in the next eight ingredients. Bring to a boil. Reduce heat; cover and simmer 20 minutes.

2 In a microwave, heat tortillas in batches until warm. Spoon 3 to 4 tablespoons of beef mixture off center on each tortilla. Sprinkle each with 2 to 3 tablespoons cheese and roll up.

BUILD-YOUR-OWN CRACKERS

I cut up deli meats and cheeses into little shapes and pack them for lunch along with assorted crackers. This is less expensive than prepackaged assortments, and children always get their favorite selections!

JACKIE RILEY, HOLLAND, MICHIGAN

hot dog bean soup

Mary Ann Kime, Sturgis, Michigan

My husband fixed this soup for our three kids years ago. They always loved it and now prepare it for their own kids. It's a real favorite on family camping trips.

- 3 hot dogs, halved lengthwise and cut into 1/4-inch pieces
- 1 teaspoon canola oil
- 1 can (16 ounces) kidney beans, rinsed and drained
- 1 can (11-1/2 ounces) condensed bean and bacon soup, undiluted
- 1-1/4 cups water
- 1 teaspoon dried minced onion
- 1/4 teaspoon pepper

1 In a large skillet, cook hot dogs in oil over medium heat for 3-4 minutes or until browned.

2 Meanwhile, in a 2-qt. microwave-safe bowl, combine the remaining ingredients. Cover and microwave on high for 2-3 minutes or until heated through, stirring once. Stir in hot dogs.

YIELD: 4 SERVINGS.

EDITOR'S NOTE: This recipe was tested in a 1,100-watt microwave.

b is for book sandwich

Taste of Home Test Kitchen

We left the bread crust on one side of the sandwich to form a book binding and cut out a letter to decorate the cover. Try making a sandwich with your child's initial for an extra-special touch.

- 12   slices bread
- 1/4   cup butter, softened
- 1/2   teaspoon minced chives
- 1/8   teaspoon onion salt
- 6   slices fully cooked ham
- 6   slices American cheese

1   Cut each slice of bread into a 3-1/2-in. x 3-1/4-in. rectangle, leaving one side with the crust on. Using a 1-1/2-in. letter cookie cutter, cut letters in half of the bread slices.

2   In a small bowl, stir the butter, chives and onion salt until blended. Spread on one side of each slice of bread. Top whole bread slices with ham and cheese; top with cutout bread.

YIELD: 6 SERVINGS.

a is for apple salad

Taste of Home Test Kitchen

This refreshing blend bursts with fruit and has a sweet dressing youngsters will find especially appealing.

- 1/2   cup sugar
- 2   tablespoons cornstarch
- 1-1/4 cups orange juice
- 1/2   teaspoon orange extract
- 1   can (20 ounces) pineapple tidbits, drained
- 1   can (11 ounces) mandarin oranges, drained
- 1   medium tart green apple, chopped
- 1   medium red apple, chopped
- 1   cup each seedless red and green grapes, halved

1   In a small saucepan, combine sugar and cornstarch. Stir in orange juice until smooth. Bring to a boil; cook and stir for 2 minutes or until thickened. Remove from heat; stir in extract. Cool.

2   In a large serving bowl, combine the pineapple, oranges, apples and grapes. Add dressing; stir gently. Cover and refrigerate until serving.

YIELD: 6 SERVINGS.

butterscotch cereal bites

Taste of Home Test Kitchen

You can make these no-bake cookies at a moment's notice for a quick snack or dessert. Plus they travel well, so you can tuck them into brown-bag lunches for a midday surprise.

2-1/2 cups miniature marshmallows
  1 cup butterscotch chips
1/4 cup peanut butter
  2 tablespoons butter
  3 cups Cheerios
1/2 cup raisins
1/2 cup flaked coconut

1 In a large heavy saucepan, combine the marshmallows, chips, peanut butter and butter. Cook and stir over medium-low heat until chips and marshmallows are melted. Remove from the heat; stir in Cheerios, raisins and coconut.

2 Drop by 1/4 cupfuls onto waxed paper. Let stand until set.

YIELD: 14-16 COOKIES.

tuna cheese spread

Dorothy Anderson, Ottawa, Kansas

The flavor of tuna is very subtle in this thick and creamy spread. It's terrific on crackers or carrot and celery sticks, stuffed in a tomato or used for a sandwich.

  1 package (8 ounces) cream cheese, softened
1/2 cup thinly sliced green onions
1/4 cup mayonnaise
  1 tablespoon lemon juice
3/4 teaspoon curry powder
Dash salt
  1 can (6 ounces) tuna, drained and flaked
Bread *or* crackers

1 In a large bowl, combine the first six ingredients. Stir in tuna. Serve with bread or crackers.

YIELD: 2 CUPS.

egg salad burritos

Sarah Inglis, Wappingers Falls, New York

When I visited Mexico, I was inspired by the fresh flavors of the food. Tomatillos and limes were widely used, and they add a tangy punch to this egg salad.

1/4 cup mayonnaise
2 teaspoons minced fresh cilantro
1 tablespoon lime juice
1/4 teaspoon cayenne pepper, optional
1/8 teaspoon salt
Dash pepper
4 hard-cooked eggs, chopped
2 whole wheat tortillas (8 inches)
1 medium tomato, thinly sliced
1 medium tomatillo, husks removed, rinsed and thinly sliced

1 In large bowl, combine the mayonnaise, cilantro, lime juice, cayenne if desired, salt and pepper. Stir in eggs.

2 Layer tortillas with tomato, tomatillo and egg salad mixture. Fold sides and ends over filling and roll up.

YIELD: 2 SERVINGS.

PACKIN' SNACKS

At the start of each week, I portion raisins, cookies, crackers, carrot sticks, orange slices and other snacks into little plastic bags. I keep them on the counter and in the fridge. When it comes time to pack daily lunches for my preschoolers, I just grab whatever snacks they need, add a sandwich and I'm done. This saves time and money, too, because I'm not buying expensive packaged snacks.

KATHY LEWIS, WARWICK, RHODE ISLAND

make-ahead s'mores

(pictured at left)

Anne Sherman, Orangeburg, South Carolina

These are perfect little desserts to keep on hand for after school or when unexpected company drops in. Young people especially like these.

- 8 ounces semisweet chocolate, chopped
- 1 can (14 ounces) sweetened condensed milk
- 1 teaspoon vanilla extract
- 16 whole graham crackers, halved
- 2 cups miniature marshmallows

1 In a heavy saucepan, melt chocolate over low heat. Add milk; cook and stir until smooth. Stir in vanilla. Making one s'more at a time, spread two graham cracker halves with one tablespoon each of chocolate mixture.

2 Place eight or nine marshmallows on one cracker; gently press the other cracker on top. Repeat. Wrap in plastic wrap; store at room temperature.

YIELD: 16 S'MORES.

blt pita pockets

Stacie Lehnen, Youngsville, Pennsylvania

I often prepare sandwiches for dinner in summer when I want to keep my kitchen cool. Pita pockets are a nice change from regular bread.

- 1 package (2.1 ounces) ready-to-serve fully cooked bacon
- 2 cups torn romaine
- 1-1/2 cups (6 ounces) shredded part-skim mozzarella cheese
- 1 large tomato, chopped
- 1/3 cup mayonnaise
- 3 pita breads (6 inches), warmed and halved
- 12 slices tomato

1 Microwave bacon according to package directions. Meanwhile, in a large bowl, combine the romaine, cheese and chopped tomato. Crumble bacon over the top; add mayonnaise and toss to coat.

2 Line pita halves with tomato slices; fill each with 1/2 cup bacon mixture.

YIELD: 6 SERVINGS.

pineapple cooler

Michelle Blumberg, Littlerock, California

A hint of lemon juice cuts the sweetness you might expect from pineapple juice and lemon-lime soda in this fun-to-drink treat.

- 1 cup unsweetened pineapple juice, chilled
- 1 to 2 tablespoons lemon juice
- 1 can (12 ounces) lemon-lime soda, chilled
- Ice cubes

1 Combine all ingredients in a pitcher. Serve the cooler over ice.

YIELD: 2-2/3 CUPS.

BROWN-BAG ICE CREAM

I fill a short thermos with ice cream or sherbet and store it in the freezer. Packed with lunch in the morning, it'll still be thick and creamy come lunchtime!

LEONA LEUCKING, WEST BURLINGTON, IOWA

lunch box apple dip

Shelly Korell, Bayard, Nebraska

Apples become an even more "a-peeling" snack when paired with this sweet, creamy dip. It's a fun and flavorful way to get kids to eat fruit.

- 1 package (8 ounces) cream cheese, softened
- 1 cup packed brown sugar
- 1 teaspoon vanilla extract
- 1 teaspoon lemon juice
- 3 to 4 apples, cut into wedges

1 In a large bowl, beat the first four ingredients until smooth. Divide into 1/3 to 1/2-cup servings and store in individual containers in the refrigerator. Serve with apples.

YIELD: 3-4 SERVINGS.

thirst-quenching limeade

Taste of Home Test Kitchen

Here is a sensational drink to quench your thirst on hot summer days. The combination of fresh, tangy lemon and lime is perfect!

5-1/2 cups water, *divided*
1-1/4 cups sugar
- 3/4 cup lemon juice (about 4 lemons)
- 3/4 cup lime juice (about 4 limes)
- 1 teaspoon grated lemon peel
- 1 teaspoon grated lime peel
Ice cubes

1 In a large saucepan, bring 1-1/2 cups water and sugar to a boil. Reduce heat; simmer, uncovered, for 10 minutes. Cool to room temperature.

2 Transfer to a 2-qt. pitcher. Stir in the juices and peels. Refrigerate for at least 1 hour. Stir in the remaining water. Serve the limeade over ice.

YIELD: 7 SERVINGS (1-3/4 QUARTS).

savory ham wraps

Ruth Peterson, Jenison, Michigan

The tasty dressing is what makes these ham and Swiss wraps so special. They're so easy to make, and if you don't have tortilla wraps, the ingredients go nicely with good home-style bread, too.

- 1/4 cup mayonnaise
- 1 tablespoon milk
- 3/4 teaspoon sugar
- 1/4 teaspoon prepared mustard
- 1/8 teaspoon celery seed
Dash salt
- 2 flour tortillas (10 inches), room temperature
- 1/4 pound thinly sliced deli ham
- 1/3 cup shredded Swiss cheese
- 2/3 cup shredded lettuce
- 1 medium tomato, seeded and chopped
- 1 green onion, chopped

1 In a small bowl, whisk the first six ingredients; spread evenly over each tortilla. Layer with ham and cheese. Top with lettuce, tomato and onion. Roll up tightly; secure with toothpicks if desired.

YIELD: 2 SERVINGS.

mini subs

Melissa Tatum
Greensboro, North Carolina

I made these sandwiches for my daughter when we ran out of bread one day. Now she prefers them this way. There's no crust!

3 tablespoons mayonnaise
4 hot dog buns, split

4 slices process American cheese
1/4 pound sliced deli ham
1/4 pound sliced deli turkey
4 slices tomato, halved
1 cup shredded lettuce

1 Spread mayonnaise over bun bottoms. Layer with cheese, ham, turkey, tomato and lettuce; replace bun tops.

YIELD: 4 SERVINGS.

apricot leather

Patsy Faye Steenbock, Riverton, Wyoming

Since it isn't sticky, this tasty, nutritious snack is perfect to take along anywhere. Kids will want to share it with all of their friends.

- 8 ounces dried apricots
- 2 tablespoons sugar
- 1 drop almond extract

Confectioners' sugar

1 Place apricots in a small saucepan and cover with water by 1 in. Bring to a boil. Reduce heat; simmer, uncovered, for 30 minutes or until soft. Drain and cool slightly.

2 Place apricots in a blender; add sugar and extract. Cover and process until smooth. Line two shallow baking pans with silicone baking mats. Spoon mixture onto mats, spreading to form two 12-in. x 8-in. rectangles.

3 Bake at 175° for 2 to 2-1/2 hours or until almost dry to the touch. Cool completely on a wire rack.

4 Transfer to a cutting board; dust both sides with confectioners' sugar. Cut into 1/2-in. x 8-in. strips; roll up. Store in an airtight container in a cool dry place.

YIELD: 4 DOZEN PIECES.

EDITOR'S NOTE: If baked fruit sticks to the knife, allow it to air-dry for 15-20 minutes, then slice and roll.

1. Cook pasta according to package directions; drain and rinse in cold water. In a small bowl, combine the pasta, chicken, oranges, cucumber, grapes and green onion.

2. In another bowl, whisk the vinaigrette ingredients. Drizzle over salad and toss to coat. Refrigerate salad until serving.

YIELD: 1 SERVING.

farmhouse barbecue muffins

Karen Kenney, Harvard, Illinois

The tangy barbecue sauce, fluffy biscuits and cheddar cheese make these little muffins a real treat. They're fun to eat.

- 1 tube (10 ounces) refrigerated buttermilk biscuits
- 1 pound ground beef
- 1/2 cup ketchup
- 3 tablespoons brown sugar
- 1 tablespoon cider vinegar
- 1/2 teaspoon chili powder
- 1 cup (4 ounces) shredded cheddar cheese

1. Separate dough into 10 biscuits; flatten into 5-in. circles. Press each onto the bottom and up the sides of a greased muffin cup; set aside.

2. In a skillet, cook beef over medium heat until no longer pink; drain. In a small bowl, combine the ketchup, brown sugar, vinegar and chili powder. Add to meat and mix well.

3. Divide the meat mixture among biscuit-lined muffin cups, using about 1/4 cup for each. Sprinkle with cheese. Bake at 375° for 18-20 minutes or until golden brown. Cool for 5 minutes before serving.

YIELD: 10 SERVINGS.

orange chicken pasta salad

Mary L. Lewis, Norman, Oklahoma

Refreshing fruits teamed with pasta, chicken and crispy veggies make a perfect single-serving salad that teenagers will enjoy.

- 1/2 cup uncooked spiral pasta
- 1/2 cup cubed cooked chicken breast
- 1/4 cup mandarin oranges
- 1/4 cup chopped cucumber
- 1/4 cup halved seedless red grapes
- 1 green onion, sliced

ORANGE VINAIGRETTE:

- 3 tablespoons orange juice concentrate
- 1 tablespoon white vinegar
- 1 tablespoon olive oil

PERFECT CAKE When I was in grade school, my mother often packed a piece of sheet cake in my lunch. When I mentioned that the icing always stuck to the plastic wrap, Mother began cutting the cake in half horizontally. She then placed the bottom half of the cake on top of the icing and the problem was solved.

MERRYBELL LOESEL, WALNUT CREEK, CALIFORNIA

vegetarian hummus wraps

(pictured at right)

Amber Indra, Thousand Oaks, California

I created this recipe mainly to help get more veggies into my diet. I'm busy and on the go like many other mothers. These wraps give me energy and taste delicious.

 6 tablespoons hummus
 2 flour tortillas (8 inches), room temperature
 1/2 cup shredded carrots
 1 cup fresh baby spinach
 6 slices tomato
 2 tablespoons green goddess salad dressing

1 Spread hummus over each tortilla. Layer with carrots, spinach and tomato; drizzle with dressing. Roll up tightly.

YIELD: 2 SERVINGS.

pita pocket chicken salad

Natasha Randall, Austin, Texas

We wanted something cool for lunch one summer day, so I tossed together whatever I had in the refrigerator. This wonderful salad was the result. People enjoy the sweet grapes, tender chicken and crunchy almonds—and they always ask for the recipe.

 2 cups cubed cooked chicken
1-1/2 cups seedless red grapes, halved
 1 cup chopped cucumber
 3/4 cup sliced almonds
 3/4 cup shredded part-skim mozzarella cheese
 1/2 cup poppy seed salad dressing
 6 pita pocket halves
Leaf lettuce, optional

1 In a large bowl, combine the chicken, grapes, cucumber, almonds and cheese. Drizzle with dressing and toss to coat. Line pita breads with lettuce if desired; fill with chicken salad.

YIELD: 6 SERVINGS.

star sandwiches

Pam Lancaster, Willis, Virginia

A simple, well-seasoned egg salad makes these star-shaped sandwiches a hit, especially during the holidays. You can use whatever bread you like, but I prefer the pretty yellow color of egg bread.

 1/2 cup mayonnaise
 1 teaspoon Dijon mustard
 1/4 teaspoon dill weed
 1/8 teaspoon salt
 1/8 teaspoon pepper
 4 hard-cooked eggs, diced
 16 slices egg bread *or* white bread

1 In a large bowl, combine the mayonnaise, mustard, dill, salt and pepper. Stir in eggs.

2 Using a large star-shaped cookie cutter, cut out 16 stars from bread. Spread half with egg salad; top with remaining bread.

YIELD: 8 SANDWICHES.

roasted pepper 'n' egg salad sandwiches

Ruby Williams, Bogalusa, Louisiana

Here's a fresh take on a classic sandwich. The egg salad gets an extra boost from red peppers and zesty seasonings.

- 1/4 cup mayonnaise
- 2 tablespoons diced roasted sweet red pepper
- 1 tablespoon minced fresh parsley
- 1/2 teaspoon Dijon mustard
- 1/2 teaspoon dried oregano
- 1/8 teaspoon pepper
- 3 hard-cooked eggs, chopped
- 4 slices multigrain bread
- 2 romaine leaves

1 In a small bowl, combine the first six ingredients. Add eggs; stir gently to combine. Spread over two slices of bread. Top with romaine and remaining bread.

YIELD: 2 SERVINGS.

ALL PLAY

With two children in elementary school, I pack 10 lunches a week. The "same old, same old" gets boring for them to eat and for me to make. To mix things up, I pack foods to let them make a cute bug. I include a poem like this: "In your lunch, you will find the parts to build a bug of some kind. With celery antennae and wings of cheese, build a butterfly if you please."

SANDY KLOSKOWSKI, ELMHURST, ILLINOIS

veggie chicken wraps

Jolene Britten, Gig Harbor, Washington

I got the idea for these wraps from a lunch I had at a cafe. During warmer months, I make them for picnics in the park. I also like to prepare a large batch, cut them into slices and serve them on a platter.

- 1 carton (8 ounces) spreadable garden vegetable cream cheese
- 4 flour tortillas (8 inches)
- 2 cups shredded romaine
- 2 small tomatoes, thinly sliced
- 8 slices provolone cheese
- 1 small red onion, thinly sliced
- 2 cups diced cooked chicken

1 Spread cream cheese evenly over each tortilla. Layer with romaine, tomatoes, cheese, onion and chicken. Roll up tightly. Cut wraps in half to serve.

YIELD: 4 SERVINGS.

crunchy tuna turnovers

Denise Hollebeke, Penhold, Alberta

I used to work with a cook who considered this sandwich one of his specialties. Once I tried it, I could see why. It's a great change from a traditional tuna sandwich. Potato chips make it fun!

- 2 cans (6 ounces each) tuna, drained and flaked
- 1/2 cup shredded cheddar cheese
- 1/3 cup mayonnaise
- 1/3 cup sliced ripe olives
- 1/8 to 1/4 teaspoon lemon-pepper seasoning
- 1 tube (12 ounces) refrigerated buttermilk biscuits
- 1 egg, beaten
- 1-1/4 cups crushed potato chips

1 In a small bowl, combine tuna, cheese, mayonnaise, olives and lemon pepper; set aside. On a lightly floured surface, flatten each biscuit into a 5-in. circle. Spoon 2 rounded tablespoonfuls of tuna mixture onto one side of each circle. Fold dough over filling; press edges with a fork to seal.

2 Place egg and potato chips in separate shallow bowls. Dip turnovers in egg, then coat with chips. Place on an ungreased baking sheet. Make a 2-1/2-in. slit in top of each turnover. Bake at 375° for 18-21 minutes or until golden brown.

YIELD: 10 SERVINGS.

wagon wheel chili

Lora Scroggins, El Dorado, Arkansas

Youngsters are sure to love the fun shape of the wagon wheel pasta in this zippy chili. It's easy to whip up with canned chili and tomato sauce, so it's great for a hot lunch or quick dinner.

- 2 cups uncooked wagon wheel *or* spiral pasta
- 1 can (15 ounces) chili
- 1 can (8 ounces) tomato sauce
- 3 tablespoons ketchup
- 1/2 teaspoon chili powder
Shredded cheddar cheese, optional

1 Cook pasta according to package directions. Meanwhile, in a large saucepan, combine the chili, tomato sauce, ketchup and chili powder. Heat through.

2 Drain and rinse pasta; stir into chili. Garnish with cheese if desired.

YIELD: 3-4 SERVINGS.

egg salad pockets

(pictured at left)

Karen Ann Bland, Gove, Kansas

Here's a delectable and filling sandwich that's perfect for packing. It doesn't get soggy because you line the pita pockets with lettuce before adding the egg salad.

1	package (3 ounces) cream cheese, softened
1/4	cup Miracle Whip
1	celery rib, finely chopped
2	tablespoons finely chopped onion
1	tablespoon sweet pickle relish
3/4	teaspoon dill weed
1/2	teaspoon salt
1/2	teaspoon ground mustard
6	hard-cooked eggs, chopped
3	pita breads (6 inches), halved
6	lettuce leaves

1 In a small bowl, combine cream cheese and Miracle Whip. Add the celery, onion, relish, dill, salt and mustard. Gently stir in eggs. Line pita halves with lettuce; fill each with 1/2 cup egg salad.

YIELD: 3 SERVINGS.

quick pizza soup

Penny Lanxon, Newell, Iowa

My kids first sampled this soup in the school cafeteria. They couldn't stop talking about it, so I knew I had to get the recipe. It's quick and easy to make.

1	pound ground beef
2	cans (26 ounces each) condensed tomato soup, undiluted

6-1/2 cups water

1 jar (28 ounces) spaghetti sauce

1	tablespoon Italian seasoning
2	cups (8 ounces) shredded cheddar cheese

Additional shredded cheddar cheese, optional

1 In a soup kettle or Dutch oven, cook beef over medium heat until no longer pink; drain. Add soup, water, spaghetti sauce and Italian seasoning; bring to a boil.

2 Reduce heat; simmer, uncovered, for 15 minutes. Add cheese; cook and stir until melted. Garnish with additional cheese if desired.

YIELD: 16 SERVINGS (4 QUARTS).

CUTE SANDWICHES

To perk up my three sons' lunches, I use large cookie cutters in seasonal shapes to make their sandwiches and pack them in decorated resealable plastic bags. My 4-year-old especially likes sandwiches in the shapes of hearts, clover leaves and eggs. He loves the fact that the bread crust is trimmed away!

KELLY WARD HARTMAN, CAPE CORAL, FLORIDA

pumpkin hot pockets

Taste of Home Test Kitchen

The simple ingredients in these hand-held sandwiches are sure to please the kids come fall.

- 1 package (15 ounces) refrigerated pie pastry
- 3 tablespoons honey mustard
- 1/2 pound fully cooked ham, thinly sliced
- 3 tablespoons thinly sliced green onions
- 1/2 cup shredded Swiss cheese
- 1/2 cup shredded Monterey Jack cheese
- 2 egg yolks
- 4 to 6 drops red food coloring
- 1 egg white
- 2 to 3 drops green food coloring

1 On a lightly floured surface, roll one sheet of pastry into a 15-in. circle. Using a floured 5-in. x 4-in. pumpkin cookie cutter, cut out eight pumpkins. Repeat with remaining pastry. Spread mustard over eight pumpkins. Layer with ham, onions and cheeses to within 3/4 in. of edges.

2 In a small bowl, beat yolks with enough red food coloring to achieve an orange color. In another small bowl, beat egg white with green food coloring. Brush orange mixture over edges of pastry. Top with remaining pumpkins. Press edges to seal; cut with a pastry wheel. Brush stems with green mixture and pumpkins with orange.

3 Transfer to greased baking sheets. Bake at 400° for 15 minutes or until browned.

YIELD: 8 SERVINGS.

creamy chicken salad

(pictured at left)

Jacklyn Salgado, Omaha, Nebraska

You can serve this delightful chicken salad on bread, buns or wrapped in a tortilla. My husband likes it on crackers as a snack or on a bed of lettuce.

- 1 boneless skinless chicken breast half (6 ounces)
- 1/2 medium onion, chopped
- 1 celery rib, chopped
- 2 teaspoons chicken bouillon granules
- 1 garlic clove, minced

Dash pepper

DRESSING:

- 1/2 cup mayonnaise
- 1 to 2 tablespoons minced fresh cilantro
- 2 tablespoons finely chopped onion

Dash salt and pepper

Assorted crackers, optional

1 In a large saucepan, combine the chicken, onion, celery, bouillon, garlic and pepper; add water to cover by 1 in. Bring to a boil. Reduce heat; cover and simmer for 15-20 minutes or until a meat thermometer reads 170°. Drain, reserving the onion, celery and garlic. Shred chicken and place in a bowl; add reserved onion mixture.

2 In a small bowl, combine the mayonnaise, cilantro, onion, salt and pepper. Spoon over chicken mixture; gently stir to coat. Cover and refrigerate until chilled. Serve with crackers if desired.

YIELD: 2 SERVINGS.

delicious apple salad

Sue Gronholz, Beaver Dam, Wisconsin

This yummy fruit salad was a favorite of my great-grandmother's. My family always enjoys it, and I'm happy knowing it's good for them, too.

- 3 cups cubed Golden and Red Delicious apples (1/2-inch cubes)
- 2 tablespoons lemon juice
- 1 cup chopped celery
- 1 cup miniature marshmallows

- 2/3 cup fat-free mayonnaise
- 1/2 cup chopped pecans *or* walnuts

1 In a large bowl, toss apples with lemon juice. Add celery and marshmallows. Stir in mayonnaise, then nuts. Serve immediately or refrigerate.

YIELD: 6 SERVINGS.

yummy tuna pitas

Marge Nicol, Shannon, Illinois

I like to tuck this cheesy tuna filling into pita pockets for a fun grab-and-go lunch. The celery adds a nice crunch. These pitas are great warmed up in the microwave.

- 1 can (6 ounces) light water-packed tuna, drained and flaked
- 1/2 cup shredded cheddar cheese
- 1/3 cup chopped celery
- 2 tablespoons chopped onion
- 1/4 cup mayonnaise
- 1 pita bread (6 inches), halved

1 In a small bowl, combine the tuna, cheese, celery, onion and mayonnaise. Spoon into pita halves. Warm in the microwave if desired.

YIELD: 2 SERVINGS.

1 stewing chicken (about 6 pounds), cut up
8 cups water
1 large onion, quartered
1 cup chopped fresh parsley
1 celery rib, sliced
5 teaspoons chicken bouillon granules
5 whole peppercorns
4 whole cloves
1 bay leaf
2 teaspoons salt
1/2 teaspoon pepper
Dash dried thyme
2 medium carrots, thinly sliced

NOODLES:
1-1/4 cups all-purpose flour
1/2 teaspoon salt
1 egg
2 tablespoons milk

1 In a stockpot, combine the first 12 ingredients; bring to a boil. Reduce heat; cover and simmer for 2-1/2 hours or until chicken is tender.

2 Remove chicken from pot. When cool enough to handle, remove meat from bones; discard bones. Cut meat into bite-size pieces. Strain broth and skim fat; return to pot. Add chicken and carrots.

3 For noodles, in a small bowl, combine flour and salt. Make a well in the center. Beat egg and milk; pour into well. Stir together, forming a dough.

4 Turn dough onto a floured surface; knead 8-10 times. Roll into a 12-in. x 9-in. rectangle. Cut into 1/2-in. strips; cut the strips into 1-in. pieces. Bring soup to a simmer; add noodles. Cover and cook for 12-15 minutes or until noodles are tender.

YIELD: 10-12 SERVINGS.

hearty chicken noodle soup

Cindy Renfrow, Sussex, New Jersey

These wonderful old-fashioned noodles give chicken soup a delightful down-home flavor. No one can resist this one!

YOU'RE SO SPECIAL!

When our three kids were in elementary school, I rarely let a day go by without including a little extra something in their lunch bags. At the very least, it was an "I love you" note written on their napkins. Sometimes I'd write a riddle for them to figure out. On their birthdays, I would wrap each food item in festive paper and ribbons. That let everyone know it was a special day!

KAREN BUHR, GASPORT, NEW YORK

speedy lunch wraps

Mary Roberts, New York Mills, Minnesota

This is such a yummy quick lunch. I served one to my sister and a week later she told me that her husband and kids couldn't stop raving about them!

- 2 tablespoons spreadable garden vegetable cream cheese
- 2 flavored tortillas of your choice (8 inches)

- 3 thin slices deli turkey (1/2 ounce *each*)
- 1/4 cup shredded lettuce
- 2 tablespoons shredded cheddar cheese
- 2 teaspoons finely chopped onion
- 2 teaspoons finely chopped green pepper
- 2 teaspoons chopped ripe olives
- 4 teaspoons ranch salad dressing

1 Spread cream cheese over tortillas. Layer with turkey, lettuce, cheese, onion, green pepper and olives; drizzle with dressing. Roll up tightly; wrap in plastic wrap. Refrigerate until serving.

YIELD: 2 SERVINGS.

hamburger noodle soup

Judy Brander, Two Harbors, Minnesota

This comfort-food classic combines ground beef with onions, celery and carrots. It's a wonderful, fast soup to make any day of the week.

1-1/2 pounds lean ground beef (90% lean)
1/2 cup *each* chopped onion, celery and carrot
7 cups water
1 envelope au jus mix
2 tablespoons beef bouillon granules
2 bay leaves
1/8 teaspoon pepper
1-1/2 cups uncooked egg noodles

1 In a large saucepan, cook the beef, onion, celery and carrot over medium heat until meat is no longer pink; drain.

2 Add the water, au jus mix, bouillon, bay leaves and pepper; bring to a boil. Stir in the noodles. Return to a boil. Cook, uncovered, for 15 minutes or until noodles are tender, stirring occasionally. Discard bay leaves.

YIELD: 8 SERVINGS (2 QUARTS).

1. Divide ham into eight portions. Top each stack with a slice of cheese. Spread both sides of bread with mayonnaise; place one slice of bread on each stack. If necessary, trim ham to fit bread.

2. Place pickle in center of each. Roll up tightly; wrap in plastic wrap. Refrigerate overnight.

YIELD: 8 SANDWICHES.

bacon egg salad croissants

Julee Wallberg, Reno, Nevada

Here's a great way to jazz up an old favorite. Egg salad gets a boost from bacon and crunchy celery.

- 1/3 cup diced celery
- 1/3 cup mayonnaise
- 1 teaspoon prepared mustard
- 1/4 teaspoon salt
- 1/8 teaspoon pepper
- 6 hard-cooked eggs, chopped
- 1/3 cup crumbled cooked bacon
- 4 lettuce leaves
- 4 thin tomato slices
- 4 croissants, split

1. In a large bowl, combine the celery, mayonnaise, mustard, salt and pepper. Stir in eggs and bacon. Place a lettuce leaf, tomato slice and 1/2 cup egg salad on each croissant.

YIELD: 4 SERVINGS.

inside-out sandwiches

Paula Truksa, Jewett, Texas

We travel a lot, and I want my family to eat right while we're away from home, so I pack a cooler full of these fun sandwiches. You can use different luncheon meats and cheeses, sweet or sour pickles and white or wheat bread to suit your tastes.

- 1 package (6 ounces) thinly sliced deli ham
- 8 slices process American cheese
- 8 slices thin sandwich bread, crusts removed
- 1/2 cup mayonnaise
- 8 dill pickle spears, well drained

CHEERFUL BANANA

If my children are tired or sad as they get ready for school, I draw a smiling face on the banana I put in their lunch bags. Sometimes I add a few words of encouragement, as if the banana were talking to them.

DARLENE OHR, CINCINNATI, OHIO

family-favorite dinners

stir into vegetable mixture. Bring to a boil; cook and stir 2 minutes or until thickened. Stir in the chicken, peas and pepper. Transfer to four 16-oz. ramekins.

3 Divide dough into four portions. On a lightly floured surface, roll out dough to fit ramekins. Place dough over chicken mixture; trim and seal edges. Cut out a decorative center or cut slits in pastry. Brush with egg white.

4 Place ramekins on a baking sheet. Bake at 425° for 20-25 minutes or until crusts are golden brown.

YIELD: 4 SERVINGS.

makeover chicken potpies

John Slivon, Navarre Beach, Florida

These individual potpies offer comforting flavor in every bite. Cut through the flaky, golden homemade crust to a rich, creamy broth brimming with hearty vegetables and juicy chunks of chicken.

- 1 cup plus 2 tablespoons all-purpose flour, *divided*
- 1/4 teaspoon baking powder
- 1/4 teaspoon salt
- 3 tablespoons cold butter, *divided*
- 2 tablespoons buttermilk
- 1 tablespoon canola oil
- 1 to 2 tablespoons cold water
- 4 medium carrots, sliced
- 3 celery ribs, sliced
- 1 large onion, chopped
- 2-1/2 cups reduced-sodium chicken broth
- 2/3 cup fat-free milk
- 2 cups cubed cooked chicken breast
- 1 cup frozen peas
- 1/8 teaspoon pepper
- 1 egg white

1 Combine 3/4 cup flour, baking powder and salt. Cut in 2 tablespoons butter until crumbly. Add buttermilk and oil; toss with a fork. Gradually add water, tossing with a fork until dough forms a ball. Cover and refrigerate for 1 hour.

2 For filling, in a large skillet, melt remaining butter. Add carrots, celery and onion; saute until crisp-tender. In a small bowl, combine remaining flour with the broth and milk until smooth. Gradually

ravioli with sausage

Krendi Ford, Belleville, Michigan

My family just loves this dish. It is on our menu at least once a month. I usually serve the ravioli with green beans and garlic bread.

- 4 cups frozen cheese ravioli (about 12 ounces)
- 1/2 pound smoked sausage, sliced
- 1 cup chopped green pepper
- 1 jar (26 ounces) meatless spaghetti sauce
- 1/4 cup shredded Parmesan cheese

1 Cook ravioli according to package directions. Meanwhile, in a large skillet, cook sausage and green pepper until meat is no longer pink. Stir in spaghetti sauce; heat through. Drain ravioli; toss with sausage mixture. Sprinkle with cheese.

YIELD: 5 SERVINGS.

green beans with bacon

Mari Anne Warren, Milton, Wisconsin

Bits of bacon and onion dress up the green beans in this easy-to-prepare side dish. These beans lend a crisp, fresh flavor to any meal.

  4   bacon strips, diced
1/2   cup chopped onion
  8   cups fresh green beans, trimmed
1/4   teaspoon salt
1/8   teaspoon pepper

1 In a large skillet, cook bacon and onion over medium heat until bacon is crisp and onion is tender. Drain.

2 Meanwhile, place beans in a large saucepan and cover with water. Bring to a boil. Cook, uncovered, for 8-10 minutes or until crisp-tender; drain well. Add to bacon mixture. Sprinkle with salt and pepper; toss to coat.

YIELD: 8 SERVINGS.

three-cheese shells

June Barrus, Springville, Utah

Here is a satisfying meatless entree that the whole family will enjoy. You can assemble the casseroles ahead and refrigerate them until ready to use. Let them stand on the counter for 30 minutes before placing in the preheated oven.

  1   package (12 ounces) jumbo pasta shells
  3   cups (24 ounces) ricotta cheese
  3   cups (12 ounces) shredded part-skim mozzarella cheese
1/2   cup grated Parmesan cheese
1/2   cup chopped green pepper
1/2   cup chopped fresh mushrooms
  2   tablespoons dried basil
  2   eggs, lightly beaten
  2   garlic cloves, minced
1/2   teaspoon seasoned salt
1/4   teaspoon pepper
  2   jars (one 28 ounces, one 14 ounces) spaghetti sauce, *divided*

1 Cook pasta shells according to package directions. Drain and rinse in cold water. In a large bowl, combine the next 10 ingredients. Divide the small jar of spaghetti sauce between two ungreased 13-in. x 9-in. baking dishes.

2 Stuff shells with the cheese mixture and place in a single layer over sauce. Pour the remaining spaghetti sauce over shells.

3 Cover and bake at 350° for 20 minutes. Uncover; bake 10 minutes longer or until heated through.

YIELD: 9 SERVINGS.

crispy chicken fingers

Rachel Fizel, Woodbury, Minnesota

My kids love these tender, moist chicken strips! My husband and I cut up the chicken and add it to salad with eggs, tomatoes and cheese. Then the whole family's happy!

- 1 cup all-purpose flour
- 1 cup dry bread crumbs
- 2 tablespoons grated Parmesan cheese
- 1 teaspoon salt
- 3/4 teaspoon garlic powder
- 1/2 teaspoon baking powder
- 1 egg
- 1 cup buttermilk
- 1-3/4 pounds boneless skinless chicken breasts, cut into strips

Oil for deep-fat frying

1 In a large resealable plastic bag, combine the first six ingredients. In a shallow bowl, whisk egg and buttermilk. Dip a few pieces of chicken at a time in buttermilk mixture, then place in bag; seal and shake to coat.

2 In an electric skillet, heat oil to 375°. Fry chicken, a few strips at a time, for 2-3 minutes on each side or until no longer pink. Drain on paper towels.

YIELD: 7 SERVINGS.

herbed chicken and tomatoes

(pictured at left)

Rebecca Popke, Largo, Florida

I put a tangy spin on chicken by adding just a few easy ingredients. Recipes such as this are really a plus when you work full time but still want to put a healthy, satisfying meal on the table.

- 1 pound boneless skinless chicken breasts, cut into 1-1/2-inch pieces
- 2 cans (14-1/2 ounces *each*) Italian diced tomatoes
- 1 envelope savory herb with garlic soup mix
- 1/4 teaspoon sugar
- Hot cooked pasta
- Shredded Parmesan cheese

1 In a 3-qt. slow cooker, combine the chicken, tomatoes, soup mix and sugar. Cover and cook on low for 5-6 hours or until chicken is no longer pink. Serve with pasta; sprinkle with cheese.

YIELD: 4 SERVINGS.

burrito pita pockets

Laura Mahaffey, Annapolis, Maryland

These little pockets are quick, delicious and kid-friendly. They're a nice eat-and-run entree for busy evenings.

- 1 pound lean ground beef (90% lean)
- 1 envelope burrito seasoning
- 1 cup water
- 1 can (2-1/4 ounces) sliced ripe olives, drained
- 4 pita pocket halves
- 1 cup shredded lettuce
- 1 medium tomato, seeded and chopped
- 3/4 cup shredded reduced-fat cheddar cheese

1 In a large nonstick skillet coated with cooking spray, cook beef over medium heat until no longer pink; drain. Stir in burrito seasoning and water. Bring to a boil. Reduce heat; simmer, uncovered, for 3-5 minutes or until thickened. Stir in olives.

2 Fill pita pockets with beef mixture, lettuce, tomato and cheese.

YIELD: 4 SERVINGS.

vegetable herb medley

Taryn Kuebelbeck, Plymouth, Minnesota

This pretty medley is dressed for a special at-home dinner with flecks of basil and thyme. It's the perfect side for grilled chicken or fish. A young cook could make the vegetables while you focus on the main dish.

- 1 package (16 ounces) frozen waxed beans, green beans and carrots
- 2 tablespoons water
- 1/4 to 1/2 teaspoon dried thyme
- 1/4 to 1/2 teaspoon dried basil
- 1/4 teaspoon salt
- 1/4 teaspoon pepper
- 2 teaspoons olive oil
- 1/2 teaspoon white wine vinegar

1 Place vegetables and water in a microwave-safe bowl. Cover and microwave on high for 9-11 minutes or until vegetables are tender.

2 Meanwhile, combine the thyme, basil, salt and pepper. Drain vegetables; drizzle with oil and vinegar. Sprinkle with seasoning mixture and toss to coat.

YIELD: 4 SERVINGS.

EDITOR'S NOTE: This recipe was tested in a 1,100-watt microwave.

3 Cover and cook on low for 4-5 hours or until heated through. Serve with spaghetti.

YIELD: 10-12 SERVINGS.

peachy sweet potatoes

Josie Bochek, Sturgeon Bay, Wisconsin

The microwave makes this special side a cinch to prepare. Juicy slices of fresh peach with cinnamon-sugar turn ordinary sweet potatoes into a standout recipe.

- 4 medium sweet potatoes
- 1 medium peach, peeled and chopped
- 3 tablespoons butter
- 2 tablespoons cinnamon-sugar

Dash salt

- 3 tablespoons chopped pecans, toasted

1 Scrub and pierce potatoes; place on a microwave-safe plate. Microwave, uncovered, on high for 10-12 minutes or until tender, turning once.

2 Meanwhile, in a small saucepan, combine the peach, butter, cinnamon-sugar and salt; bring to a boil. Cook and stir for 2-3 minutes or until the peach is tender. Cut an "X" in the top of each potato; fluff pulp with a fork. Spoon peach mixture into each potato. Sprinkle with pecans.

YIELD: 4 SERVINGS.

EDITOR'S NOTE: This recipe was tested in a 1,100-watt microwave.

mom's spaghetti sauce

Kristy Hawkes, South Ogden, Utah

Mom made this when we were kids, and it was always my first choice for birthday dinners. Now I do the prep work in the morning and just let it simmer all day. When I get home, all I have to do is boil the spaghetti, brown some garlic bread and dinner is on!

- 1 pound ground beef
- 1 medium onion, chopped
- 1 medium green pepper, chopped
- 8 to 10 fresh mushrooms, sliced
- 3 celery ribs, chopped
- 1-1/2 teaspoons minced garlic
- 2 cans (14-1/2 ounces *each*) Italian stewed tomatoes
- 1 jar (26 ounces) spaghetti sauce
- 1/2 cup ketchup
- 2 teaspoons brown sugar
- 1 teaspoon sugar
- 1 teaspoon salt
- 1 teaspoon dried oregano
- 1 teaspoon chili powder
- 1 teaspoon prepared mustard

Hot cooked spaghetti

1 In a large skillet, cook the beef, onion, green pepper, mushrooms and celery over medium heat until meat is no longer pink. Add garlic; cook 1 minute longer. Drain.

2 In a 3-qt. slow cooker, combine the tomatoes, spaghetti sauce, ketchup, sugars, salt, oregano, chili powder and mustard. Stir in the beef mixture.

pizza burgers

Mitzi Sentiff, Annapolis, Maryland

Pizza burgers are always a kid's favorite. By adding herbs and cheese to the burgers and serving them on English muffins, they've become a favorite for adults in the family as well.

1	egg, lightly beaten
3/4	cup grated Parmesan cheese
1/2	cup chopped onion
1/4	cup minced fresh parsley
3/4	teaspoon dried basil
3/4	teaspoon dried oregano
3/4	teaspoon dried rosemary, crushed

3/4	teaspoon pepper
1	pound ground beef
4	slices provolone cheese
4	English muffins, split and toasted
1/2	cup pizza sauce

1 In a large bowl, combine the first eight ingredients. Crumble beef over mixture and mix well. Shape into four patties.

2 Grill burgers, covered, over medium heat for 5-7 minutes on each side or until a meat thermometer reads 160° and juices run clear. Top with cheese; cover and grill 2-3 minutes longer or until cheese is melted. Serve burgers on muffins with pizza sauce.

YIELD: 4 SERVINGS.

honey-soy pork chops

(pictured at left)

Edie DeSpain, Logan, Utah

Summer is always a special time for relaxed and casual meals, for patriotic holidays and especially picnics in the great outdoors. This recipe is perfect for such occasions.

- 1/4 cup lemon juice
- 1/4 cup honey
- 2 tablespoons reduced-sodium soy sauce
- 1 tablespoon unsweetened apple juice
- 2 garlic cloves, minced
- 4 boneless pork loin chops (4 ounces *each*)

1 In a small bowl, combine the first five ingredients. Pour 1/2 cup into a large resealable plastic bag; add pork chops. Seal bag and turn to coat; refrigerate for 2-3 hours. Cover and refrigerate remaining marinade for basting.

2 Drain and discard marinade. Moisten a paper towel with cooking oil; using long-handled tongs, lightly coat the grill rack.

3 Grill pork, covered, over medium heat or broil 4 in. over heat for 4-5 minutes on each side or until a meat thermometer reads 160°, basting frequently with remaining marinade.

YIELD: 4 SERVINGS.

sweet 'n' sour meatballs

Andrea Busch, Brackenridge, Pennsylvania

This Asian dinner served over rice is a welcome change of pace from routine menus. My husband isn't normally a big fan of stir-fries, and our children can be picky eaters, but I never have leftovers when I serve this dish.

- 1 egg
- 1/4 cup seasoned bread crumbs
- 1/2 teaspoon salt
- 1/4 teaspoon ground ginger
- Dash pepper
- 1 pound ground beef
- 1 can (20 ounces) pineapple chunks
- 1/4 cup cider vinegar
- 1/4 cup packed brown sugar
- 2 tablespoons soy sauce
- 1 cup sliced carrots
- 1 medium green pepper, julienned
- 1 tablespoon cornstarch
- 2 tablespoons cold water
- Hot cooked rice

1 In a large bowl, combine the first five ingredients. Crumble beef over mixture and mix well. Shape into 1-in. balls. In a large skillet, cook meatballs over medium heat until no longer pink; drain.

2 Drain pineapple, reserving juice; set pineapple aside. Add water to juice to measure 1 cup. Stir in the vinegar, brown sugar and soy sauce; pour over meatballs. Add carrots. Bring to a boil. Reduce heat; cover and simmer for 5-8 minutes or until carrots are crisp-tender. Stir in green pepper and pineapple; cover and simmer 5 minutes longer or until pepper is crisp-tender.

3 Combine cornstarch and cold water until smooth; stir into the pan. Bring to a boil; cook and stir for 2 minutes or until thickened. Serve with rice.

YIELD: 4-6 SERVINGS.

1/2   teaspoon sugar
1/2   teaspoon chicken bouillon granules
1   plum tomato, chopped
2   tablespoons chopped red onion
1   cup torn iceberg lettuce
1   bacon strip, cooked and crumbled

1 Cook macaroni according to package directions; drain and rinse in cold water. In a small bowl, combine the mayonnaise, chili sauce, lemon juice, sugar and bouillon; stir in the macaroni, tomato and onion.

2 Refrigerate until chilled. Serve in a lettuce-lined bowl; sprinkle with bacon.

YIELD: 1 SERVING.

breaded pork chops

Ann Ingalls, Gladstone, Missouri

A new, zippy version of an old favorite, this pork chop recipe is guaranteed to bring your family together around the dinner table.

1   cup seasoned bread crumbs
2   tablespoons grated Parmesan cheese
1/3   cup prepared ranch salad dressing
6   bone-in pork loin chops (1/2 inch thick and 8 ounces each)

1 In a shallow bowl, combine the bread crumbs and cheese. Place dressing in another shallow bowl. Dip pork chops in dressing, then roll in crumb mixture.

2 Place in an ungreased 13-in. x 9-in. baking pan. Bake, uncovered, at 375° for 25 minutes or until a meat thermometer reads 160°.

YIELD: 6 SERVINGS.

blt in a bowl

Velma Jenness, Marcus, Iowa

This hearty pasta medley is sure to become a staple. Teens can make this for a simple dinner on their own. Or increase the recipe to feed the whole family.

1/4   cup uncooked elbow macaroni
3   tablespoons mayonnaise
4   teaspoons chili sauce
1-1/2   teaspoons lemon juice

our favorite mac & cheese

(pictured at right)

Margaret Spear, Morris, Illinois

I have forever been experimenting with macaroni and cheese. This recipe is the one my husband likes the best! You and your kids are sure to love it, too!

2-1/2 cups uncooked elbow macaroni
1/4   cup butter, cubed
1   can (12 ounces) evaporated milk
3   eggs, lightly beaten
5   slices process American cheese, chopped
1   cup (8 ounces) sour cream
3/4   cup process cheese sauce
3/4   teaspoon onion powder
1/2   teaspoon seasoned salt
1/8   teaspoon pepper
2-1/2 cups (10 ounces) shredded cheddar cheese, *divided*

1 Cook macaroni according to package directions.

2 Meanwhile, in a large saucepan, melt butter. Stir in the milk, eggs, process cheese, sour cream, cheese sauce and seasonings. Cook and stir over medium heat for 3-4 minutes or until cheeses are melted. Drain macaroni; toss with 2 cups cheddar cheese.

3 Transfer to a greased 13-in. x 9-in. baking dish. Add the sauce mixture and mix well. Sprinkle with remaining cheddar cheese. Bake, uncovered, at 350° for 35-40 minutes or until golden brown and bubbly.

YIELD: 8 SERVINGS.

steak 'n' fries salad

Nancy Collins, Clearfield, Pennsylvania

This is a popular dish at restaurants in central Pennsylvania. It makes the perfect amount for two and is great for a quiet night in.

3	tablespoons sugar
2	tablespoons canola oil
4-1/2	teaspoons malt vinegar
1-1/2	teaspoons water
1	cup frozen french fried potatoes
1/2	pound boneless beef sirloin steak, thinly sliced
3	cups shredded lettuce
1/3	cup chopped tomato
1/4	cup chopped red onion
1/2	cup shredded part-skim mozzarella cheese

1 For dressing, in a small bowl, whisk the sugar, oil, vinegar and water.

2 Prepare the french fries according to package directions. Meanwhile, in a small skillet coated with cooking spray, cook steak strips over medium heat for 6-10 minutes or until meat reaches desired doneness.

3 On two salad plates, arrange the lettuce, tomato and onion. Top with french fries, steak and cheese. Whisk dressing; drizzle over salads.

YIELD: 2 SERVINGS.

chili hot dog spaghetti

Karen Tausend, Bridgeport, Michigan

I've been making this recipe for over 35 years. It's one of my husband's favorites. Lower-fat franks and reduced-fat cheese can be used and the dish is just as good.

- 8   ounces uncooked spaghetti
- 1   package (1 pound) hot dogs, halved lengthwise and sliced
- 1/2 cup chopped onion
- 1/2 cup chopped celery
- 2   tablespoons canola oil
- 1   can (15 ounces) tomato sauce
- 1   tablespoon prepared mustard
- 1   teaspoon chili powder
- 1/2 teaspoon Worcestershire sauce
- 1/4 teaspoon salt
- 1/4 teaspoon pepper
- 1   cup (4 ounces) shredded cheddar cheese

1 Cook spaghetti according to package directions. Meanwhile, in a large skillet, saute the hot dogs, onion and celery in oil until tender. Stir in the tomato sauce, mustard, chili powder, Worcestershire sauce, salt and pepper. Cook, uncovered, for 5-8 minutes or until heated through, stirring occasionally.

2 Drain spaghetti; toss with hot dog mixture. Sprinkle with cheese.

YIELD: 6 SERVINGS.

slow cooker sloppy joes

Carol Losier, Baldwinsville, New York

On hot summer days, this cooks without heating up the kitchen while I work on the rest of the meal. It's easy to double or triple for crowds, and if there are any leftovers, you can freeze them to enjoy later!

- 1-1/2 pounds ground beef
- 1   cup chopped celery
- 1/2 cup chopped onion
- 1   bottle (12 ounces) chili sauce
- 2   tablespoons brown sugar
- 2   tablespoons sweet pickle relish
- 1   tablespoon Worcestershire sauce
- 1   teaspoon salt
- 1/8 teaspoon pepper
- 8   hamburger buns, split

1 In a large skillet, cook the beef, celery and onion over medium heat until meat is no longer pink; drain. Transfer to a 3-qt. slow cooker.

2 Stir in the chili sauce, brown sugar, pickle relish, Worcestershire sauce, salt and pepper.

3 Cover and cook on low for 3-4 hours or until flavors are blended. Serve on buns.

YIELD: 8 SERVINGS.

cheese-stuffed burgers

Janet Wood, Windham, New Hampshire

Do regular cheeseburgers one better with a fun recipe that puts the cheese, ketchup, mustard and onions inside the burger. People love biting into a hidden pocket of their favorite toppings.

1/4	cup ketchup
1/4	cup finely chopped onion
4	teaspoons prepared mustard
2	teaspoons salt
1	teaspoon pepper
4	pounds ground beef
1-1/2	cups (6 ounces) shredded cheddar cheese
12	hamburger buns, split

1 In a large bowl, combine the first five ingredients. Crumble beef over mixture and mix well. Shape into 24 thin patties. Sprinkle cheese in the center of 12 patties; top with remaining patties and press edges firmly to seal.

2 Grill, covered, over medium heat or broil 4 in. from the heat for 6-9 minutes on each side or until no longer pink. Serve on buns.

YIELD: 12 SERVINGS.

garden pizza supreme

Pamela Shank, Parkersburg, West Virginia

This pizza is so delicious and colorful. Toss any vegetables from the garden onto yours.

1	loaf (1 pound) frozen bread dough, thawed
6	slices part-skim mozzarella cheese
1	can (8 ounces) pizza sauce
2	cups (8 ounces) shredded part-skim mozzarella cheese, *divided*
1/2	cup *each* finely chopped fresh cauliflowerets, mushrooms and broccoli florets
1/4	cup *each* finely chopped red onion, green pepper and sweet red pepper
1/2	cup pickled pepper rings

1 Roll the dough into a 15-in. circle. Transfer to a greased 14-in. pizza pan, building up edges slightly. Place cheese slices on dough. Spread sauce over cheese. Sprinkle with 1 cup shredded cheese, cauliflower, mushrooms, broccoli, onion, peppers and pepper rings.

2 Bake at 425° for 15 minutes. Sprinkle with remaining cheese. Bake 5-10 minutes longer or until cheese is melted and crust is golden brown.

YIELD: 8 SLICES.

spaghetti 'n' meatballs

Mary Lou Koskella, Prescott, Arizona

One evening, we had unexpected company. Since I had some of these meatballs left over in the freezer, I warmed them up as appetizers. Everyone raved! This classic recipe makes a big batch and is perfect for entertaining.

1-1/2 cups chopped onions
2 tablespoons olive oil
3 garlic cloves, minced
3 cups water
1 can (29 ounces) tomato sauce
2 cans (12 ounces each) tomato paste
1/3 cup minced fresh parsley
1 tablespoon dried basil
1 tablespoon salt
1/2 teaspoon pepper

MEATBALLS:

4 eggs, lightly beaten
2 cups soft bread cubes (1/4-inch pieces)
1-1/2 cups milk
1 cup grated Parmesan cheese
3 garlic cloves, minced
1 tablespoon salt
1/2 teaspoon pepper
3 pounds ground beef
2 tablespoons canola oil
Hot cooked spaghetti

1 In a Dutch oven over medium heat, saute onions in oil until tender. Add garlic; cook 1 minute longer. Add the water, tomato sauce and paste, parsley, basil, salt and pepper; bring to a boil. Reduce heat; cover and simmer for 50 minutes.

2 In a large bowl, combine the first seven meatball ingredients. Crumble beef over mixture and mix well. Shape into 1-1/2-in. balls.

3 In a large skillet over medium heat, brown meatballs in oil; drain. Add to sauce; bring to a boil. Reduce heat; cover and simmer for 1 hour, stirring occasionally. Serve with spaghetti.

YIELD: 12-16 SERVINGS.

almond chicken strips

(pictured at left)

Wendy Thurston, Bow Island, Alberta

Whether I serve these nutty chicken strips as an appetizer or entree, there are never leftovers.

1/4 cup cornstarch
1 teaspoon sugar
1/2 teaspoon salt
1-1/2 teaspoons water
2 egg whites, lightly beaten
1-1/2 cups ground almonds
1 pound boneless skinless chicken breasts, cut into 1/2-inch strips
2 tablespoons canola oil
Honey mustard, optional

1 In a shallow bowl, combine the cornstarch, sugar, salt and water until smooth. Gradually stir in the egg whites. Place the almonds in another shallow bowl. Dip chicken in egg white mixture, then coat with almonds.

2 In a large skillet or wok, stir-fry chicken strips in oil for 5-7 minutes or until no longer pink; drain on paper towels. Serve with honey mustard for dipping if desired.

YIELD: 4 SERVINGS.

seasoned potato wedges

Linda Hartsell, Apple Creek, Ohio

After many years of working in a beauty shop, I have quite a collection of delicious recipes from many clients who are wonderful cooks, and this is one of my favorites. It's easy because you don't peel the potatoes.

4 medium russet potatoes
2 to 3 tablespoons mayonnaise
1 to 2 teaspoons seasoned salt

1 Cut the potatoes in half lengthwise; cut each half lengthwise into three wedges. Place in a single layer on a greased baking sheet. Spread mayonnaise over cut sides of potatoes; sprinkle with seasoned salt.

2 Bake at 350° for 50-60 minutes or until tender.

YIELD: 4 SERVINGS.

southwest beef pie

Taste of Home Test Kitchen

This meaty delight will have the family coming back for seconds! Rich and filling, it's sure to be an instant classic.

2 cups coarsely crushed nacho tortilla chips
1-1/2 pounds ground beef
1 can (8 ounces) tomato sauce
1/2 cup water
1 envelope taco seasoning
1/4 teaspoon pepper
1 cup (4 ounces) shredded Monterey Jack cheese

1 Place the tortilla chips in an ungreased 9-in. pie plate; set aside. In a large skillet, cook beef over medium heat until no longer pink; drain. Add the tomato sauce, water, taco seasoning and pepper. Bring to a boil; cook and stir for 2 minutes or until thickened.

2 Spoon half of the meat mixture over chips; sprinkle with half of the cheese. Repeat layers.

3 Bake, uncovered, at 375° for 10-15 minutes or until heated through and cheese is melted.

YIELD: 6 SERVINGS.

pigs in a blanket

Kay Curtis, Guthrie, Oklahoma

I fill hot dogs with cheese and wrap them in a light homemade dough to make them special. They are tasty, fun and handy to eat.

- 1 package (1/4 ounce) active dry yeast
- 1/3 cup plus 1 teaspoon sugar, *divided*
- 2/3 cup warm milk (110° to 115°)
- 1/3 cup warm water (110° to 115°)
- 1 egg, beaten
- 2 tablespoons plus 2 teaspoons shortening, melted
- 1 teaspoon salt
- 3-2/3 cups all-purpose flour
- 10 hot dogs
- 2 slices process American cheese

1 In a large bowl, dissolve yeast and 1 teaspoon sugar in milk and water; let stand for 5 minutes. Add the egg, shortening, salt, remaining sugar and enough flour to form a soft dough.

2 Turn onto a floured surface; knead until smooth and elastic, about 8-10 minutes. Place in a greased bowl, turning once to grease top. Cover and let rise in a warm place until doubled, about 1 hour.

3 Cut a 1/4-in.-deep lengthwise slit in each hot dog. Cut cheese slices into five strips; place one strip in a slit of each hot dog.

4 Punch dough down; divide into 10 portions. Roll each into a 5-in. x 2-1/2-in. rectangle and wrap around prepared hot dogs; pinch seams and ends to seal.

5 Place seam side down on greased baking sheets; let rise for 30 minutes. Bake at 350° for 15-18 minutes or until golden brown.

YIELD: 10 SERVINGS.

southwest chicken

(pictured at right)

Maddymoo, Taste of Home Online Community

In this recipe, chicken is cooked until tender and combined with corn, beans, cheese, and salsa for a delicious meal with Southwestern flair. The garnishes really complete the meal.

- 1 can (15-1/4 ounces) whole kernel corn, drained
- 1 can (15 ounces) black beans, rinsed and drained
- 1 jar (16 ounces) mild salsa
- 4 boneless skinless chicken breast halves (5 ounces *each*)
- Sweet red and yellow pepper strips, sour cream, shredded cheddar cheese and sliced green onions, optional

1 In a 3-qt. slow cooker, layer three-fourths each of the corn and beans and half of the salsa. Add chicken; top with remaining corn, beans and salsa. Cover and cook on low for 4-5 hours or until chicken is tender.

2 Shred chicken with two forks and return to slow cooker; heat through. Serve with toppings.

YIELD: 6 SERVINGS.

honey-glazed carrots

Judie Anglen, Riverton, Wyoming

My mother used sugar in this recipe, but a man who keeps bees on our farm shares honey with us, so I use that.

- 1 package (16 ounces) baby carrots
- 1 tablespoon water
- 2 tablespoons butter
- 2 tablespoons honey
- 1 tablespoon lemon juice

1 Place carrots and water in a 1-1/2-qt. microwave-safe dish. Cover and microwave on high for 3-5 minutes or until crisp-tender.

2 Meanwhile, melt butter in a large skillet; stir in honey and lemon juice. Cook over low heat for 3-1/2 minutes, stirring constantly. Add carrots; cook and stir for 1 minute or until glazed.

YIELD: 4 SERVINGS.

EDITOR'S NOTE: This recipe was tested in a 1,100-watt microwave.

tomato tart with three cheeses

(pictured at left)

Taste of Home Cooking School

This quick and easy recipe will delight the pizza lovers in your home. You will be surprised at how quickly it comes together.

- 1 sheet frozen puff pastry, thawed
- 3/4 cup shredded part-skim mozzarella cheese
- 3/4 cup shredded provolone cheese
- 1/4 cup minced fresh basil
- 4 plum tomatoes, thinly sliced
- Salt and pepper to taste
- 1/4 cup shredded Parmesan cheese
- Additional minced fresh basil

1 Unfold pastry sheet on a lightly floured surface. Roll into a 12-in. square; transfer to a parchment paper-lined baking sheet. Prick with a fork.

2 Combine the mozzarella cheese, provolone cheese and basil; sprinkle over the pastry to within 1 in. of edges. Arrange the tomato slices over the cheese. Season with salt and pepper; sprinkle with Parmesan cheese.

3 Bake at 400° for 15-20 minutes or until pastry is golden brown. Remove tart from baking sheet to a wire rack to cool for 5 minutes. Sprinkle tart with additional basil. Serve hot or at room temperature.

YIELD: 4 SERVINGS.

southwest tuna noodle bake

Sandra Crane, Las Cruces, New Mexico

None of my coworkers had ever tried tuna noodle casserole. Since we live near the Mexican border, they challenged me to make my version Southwestern. After trying this dish, everyone wanted the recipe!

- 1 package (16 ounces) egg noodles
- 2-1/2 cups milk
- 2 cans (6 ounces *each*) light water-packed tuna, drained
- 1 can (10-3/4 ounces) condensed cream of chicken soup, undiluted
- 1 can (10-3/4 ounces) condensed cream of mushroom soup, undiluted

- 1 cup (4 ounces) shredded cheddar cheese
- 1 can (4 ounces) chopped green chilies
- 2 cups crushed tortilla chips

1 Cook noodles according to package directions. Meanwhile, in a large bowl, combine the milk, tuna, soups, cheese and chilies. Drain noodles; gently stir into tuna mixture.

2 Transfer to an ungreased 13-in. x 9-in. baking dish. Sprinkle with tortilla chips. Bake, uncovered, at 350° for 30-35 minutes or until bubbly.

YIELD: 6 SERVINGS.

parmesan corn on the cob

Suzanne McKinley, Lyons, Georgia

Here's an easy way to season fresh corn on the cob. Your family will enjoy it.

- 1/4 cup butter, melted
- 1/4 cup grated Parmesan cheese
- 1/2 teaspoon Italian seasoning
- 4 ears corn on the cob
- 1/4 cup water
- Salt to taste

1 In a bowl, combine the butter, cheese and Italian seasoning; set aside. Remove husks and silk from corn; place corn in a shallow microwave-safe dish. Add water. Cover and microwave on high for 7-10 minutes, turning once. Let stand for 5 minutes; drain. Brush with butter mixture; sprinkle with salt.

YIELD: 4 SERVINGS.

EDITOR'S NOTE: This recipe was tested in a 1,100-watt microwave.

polenta chili casserole

Dan Kelmenson, West Bloomfield, Michigan

We created this delicious vegetarian bean and polenta bake that combines spicy chili, mixed veggies and homemade polenta. It's a warm and comfy casserole that is sure to please everyone, vegetarian or not.

1-1/4 cups yellow cornmeal
1/2 teaspoon salt
  4 cups boiling water
  2 cups (8 ounces) shredded cheddar cheese, *divided*
  3 cans (15 ounces *each*) vegetarian chili with beans
  1 package (16 ounces) frozen mixed vegetables, thawed and well drained

1 In a large saucepan, combine cornmeal and salt. Gradually whisk in boiling water. Cook and stir over medium heat for 5 minutes or until thickened. Remove from the heat. Stir in 1/4 cup cheddar cheese until melted.

2 Spread into a 13-in. x 9-in. baking dish coated with cooking spray. Bake, uncovered, at 350° for 20 minutes. Meanwhile, heat chili according to package directions.

3 Spread vegetables over polenta; top with chili. Sprinkle with remaining cheese. Bake 12-15 minutes longer or until cheese is melted. Let stand for 10 minutes before serving.

YIELD: 8 SERVINGS.

confetti mac 'n' cheese

Debbie Amacher, Amherst, New York

My family loves this rich dish, usually as a side. As long as the kids don't realize its squash, they'll keep on eating it!

1-1/2 cups uncooked elbow macaroni
  2 cups chopped zucchini
1/2 cup chopped onion
  2 tablespoons canola oil
  1 can (14-1/2 ounces) diced tomatoes, drained
  1 can (10-3/4 ounces) condensed cheddar cheese soup, undiluted
  2 cups (8 ounces) shredded cheddar cheese
1/2 cup milk
1/2 teaspoon dried basil
1/2 teaspoon prepared mustard

1 Cook macaroni according to package directions. Meanwhile, in a large saucepan, saute zucchini and onion in oil until tender. Stir in the tomatoes, soup, cheese, milk, basil and mustard.

2 Cook, uncovered, over medium heat for 6-7 minutes or until cheese is melted, stirring often. Drain macaroni; toss with vegetable cheese sauce.

YIELD: 4 SERVINGS.

zesty tacos

Susie Bonham, Fairview, Oklahoma

Jazz up everyday tacos in a snap! Black-eyed peas and a drizzle of Italian dressing are the surprise ingredients that perk up this recipe.

1　pound ground beef
1　cup water
1　envelope taco seasoning
8　taco shells
1　can (15-1/2 ounces) black-eyed peas, rinsed and drained
1　cup chopped tomatoes
1　cup shredded lettuce
1　cup (4 ounces) shredded cheddar cheese
1/2　cup zesty Italian salad dressing

1　In a large skillet, cook beef over medium heat for 5-6 minutes or until meat is no longer pink; drain. Stir in water and taco seasoning. Bring to a boil. Reduce heat; simmer, uncovered, for 4-5 minutes or until thickened.

2　Meanwhile, prepare taco shells according to package directions. Stir peas into skillet; heat through. Spoon 1/4 cup beef mixture into each taco shell. Top with tomatoes, lettuce and cheese. Drizzle with salad dressing.

YIELD: 8 SERVINGS.

bacon-cheddar meat loaves

Tonya Vowels, Vine Grove, Kentucky

It's easy to get your family eating healthier with fun little meat loaves like these. No one will guess they're light.

4 egg whites
1/2 cup crushed reduced-fat butter-flavored crackers (about 13 crackers)
1/3 cup plus 8 teaspoons shredded reduced-fat cheddar cheese, *divided*
1/4 cup chopped onion
1/2 teaspoon salt
1/4 teaspoon pepper
1 pound lean ground beef (90% lean)
2 turkey bacon strips, cut in half

1 In a large bowl, combine the egg whites, crackers, 1/3 cup cheese, onion, salt and pepper. Crumble beef over mixture and mix well. Shape into four small loaves; place in an ungreased 11-in. x 7-in. baking dish. Top each with a half-strip of bacon.

2 Bake at 350° for 35-40 minutes or until no pink remains and a meat thermometer reads 160°. Sprinkle with remaining cheese; bake 2-3 minutes longer or until cheese is melted.

YIELD: 4 SERVINGS.

black bean 'n' corn quesadillas

Susan Franklin, Littleton, Colorado

Black beans partner up with spinach and corn in these easy and satisfying quesadillas.

- 1 can (15 ounces) black beans, rinsed and drained, *divided*
- 1 small onion, finely chopped
- 2 teaspoons olive oil
- 1 can (11 ounces) Mexicorn, drained
- 1 teaspoon chili powder
- 1 teaspoon ground cumin
- 1 package (6 ounces) fresh baby spinach
- 8 flour tortillas (8 inches)
- 3/4 cup shredded reduced-fat Monterey Jack cheese or Mexican cheese blend

1 In a small bowl, mash 1 cup beans with a fork. In a large skillet, saute onion in oil until tender. Add the corn, chili powder, cumin, mashed beans and remaining beans; cook and stir until heated through. Stir in spinach just until wilted.

2 Place two tortillas on an ungreased baking sheet; spread each with a rounded 1/2 cup of bean mixture. Sprinkle each with 3 tablespoons of cheese; top with another tortilla. Repeat.

3 Bake at 400° for 8-10 minutes or until cheese is melted. Cut each quesadilla into six wedges. Serve warm.

YIELD: 6 SERVINGS.

pizza salad with tomato vinaigrette

Wendy Nickel, Kiester, Minnesota

Many of the ingredients in a deluxe pizza go into this no-hassle salad. Feel free to substitute pepperoni for the Canadian bacon. The dressing is great on other salads, too.

VINAIGRETTE:
- 1 can (8 ounces) tomato sauce
- 1/2 cup olive oil
- 1/4 cup white wine vinegar
- 1 teaspoon sugar
- 1 teaspoon dried oregano
- 1 garlic clove, minced
- 1/2 teaspoon salt

SALAD:
- 1 package (6 ounces) fresh baby spinach
- 1/2 pound Canadian bacon, cut into thin strips
- 1 cup (4 ounces) shredded part-skim mozzarella cheese
- 1 cup (4 ounces) shredded reduced-fat cheddar cheese
- 2 medium tomatoes, cut into wedges and seeded
- 1 medium green pepper, finely chopped
- 1 can (2-1/4 ounces) sliced ripe olives, drained
- 3 fresh basil leaves, thinly sliced
- 1 tablespoon minced chives

1 In a small bowl, whisk the vinaigrette ingredients. Chill until serving.

2 In a large salad bowl, combine the spinach, bacon, cheeses, tomatoes, pepper, olives, basil and chives. Just before serving, whisk dressing and drizzle 1 cup over salad; toss to coat. Save remaining dressing for another use.

YIELD: 10-1/2 CUPS SALAD PLUS 3/4 CUP LEFTOVER DRESSING.

roasted sugar snap peas

Taste of Home Test Kitchen

We're betting you won't find a faster way to dress up crisp sugar snap peas than with this scrumptious recipe. It goes with a variety of entrees and is pretty enough to dish up for company.

1 package (8 ounces) fresh sugar snap peas
1 tablespoon chopped shallot
2 teaspoons olive oil
1/2 teaspoon Italian seasoning
1/8 teaspoon salt

1 Place peas in an ungreased shallow baking pan. Combine the shallot, oil, Italian seasoning and salt; drizzle over peas and toss to coat.

2 Bake, uncovered, at 400° for 8-10 minutes or until crisp-tender, stirring once.

YIELD: 2 SERVINGS.

slow-cooked mac 'n' cheese

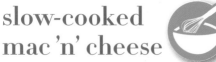

Shelby Molina, Whitewater, Wisconsin

Slow-Cooked Mac 'n' Cheese: the words alone are enough to make mouths water. This is comfort food at its best: rich and extra-cheesy. And because it's made in the slow cooker, it's easy.

2 cups uncooked elbow macaroni
1 can (12 ounces) evaporated milk
1-1/2 cups milk
1/2 cup egg substitute
1/4 cup butter, melted

1 teaspoon salt
2-1/2 cups (10 ounces) shredded cheddar cheese
2-1/2 cups (10 ounces) shredded sharp cheddar cheese, *divided*

1 Cook macaroni according to package directions; drain and rinse in cold water. In a large bowl, combine the evaporated milk, milk, egg substitute, butter and salt. Stir in the cheddar cheese, 2 cups sharp cheddar cheese and macaroni.

2 Transfer to a greased 3-qt. slow cooker. Cover and cook on low for 2-3 hours or until center is set, stirring once. Sprinkle with remaining sharp cheddar cheese.

YIELD: 9 SERVINGS.

sweet-and-sour pork

(pictured at right)

Eleanor Dunbar, Peoria, Illinois

A homemade sweet-and-sour sauce makes the difference in this yummy combo of tender pork, crunchy veggies and tangy pineapple. Serve it over hot rice, chow mein noodles or both.

2/3 cup packed brown sugar
2/3 cup cider vinegar
2/3 cup ketchup
2 teaspoons soy sauce
1 pound boneless pork loin, cut into 1-inch cubes
1 tablespoon canola oil
1 medium onion, cut into chunks
2 medium carrots, sliced
1 medium green pepper, cut into 1-inch pieces
1/2 teaspoon minced garlic
1/4 teaspoon ground ginger
1 can (8 ounces) pineapple chunks, drained
Hot cooked rice, optional

1 In a small bowl, combine the brown sugar, vinegar, ketchup and soy sauce. Pour half into a large resealable plastic bag; add pork. Seal bag and turn to coat; refrigerate for 30 minutes. Set remaining marinade aside.

2 Drain and discard marinade from pork. In a large skillet, cook pork in oil for 3 minutes. Add the onion, carrots, green pepper, garlic and ginger; saute until pork is no longer pink. Add reserved marinade. Bring to a boil; cook for 1 minute. Stir in the pineapple. Serve with rice if desired.

YIELD: 4 SERVINGS.

chili cheese dog casserole

(pictured at left)

Taste of Home Test Kitchen

Kids and parents alike will dive right into this hearty, comforting dish. With a crispy cheese topping on a warm corn bread crust, this recipe is a keeper.

- 1 package (8-1/2 ounces) corn bread/muffin mix
- 1 cup chopped green pepper
- 1/2 cup chopped onion
- 1/2 cup chopped celery
- 1 tablespoon olive oil
- 1 package (1 pound) hot dogs, halved lengthwise and cut into bite-size pieces
- 1 can (15 ounces) chili with beans
- 2 tablespoons brown sugar
- 1/2 teaspoon garlic powder
- 1/2 teaspoon chili powder
- 1 cup (4 ounces) shredded cheddar cheese, *divided*

1 Prepare corn bread batter according to package directions. Spread half of the batter into a greased 8-in. square baking dish; set aside.

2 In a large skillet, saute the green pepper, onion and celery in oil until crisp-tender. Stir in hot dogs; saute 3-4 minutes longer or until lightly browned. Stir in the chili, brown sugar, garlic powder and chili powder; heat through. Stir in 3/4 cup cheese.

3 Spoon over corn bread batter; top with remaining corn bread batter. Sprinkle remaining cheese over the top.

4 Bake, uncovered, at 350° for 28-32 minutes or until a toothpick inserted near the center comes out clean. Let stand for 5 minutes before serving.

YIELD: 6 SERVINGS.

four-cheese baked ziti

Diane Nemitz, Ludington, Michigan

A day without pasta is a like a day without sunshine! Loaded with vegetables and cheese, baked ziti will definitely make your days brighter.

- 1 cup chopped onion
- 1/2 cup chopped green pepper
- 1/2 cup shredded carrots
- 2 garlic cloves, minced
- 2 cans (14-1/2 ounces *each*) Italian diced tomatoes
- 1 can (15 ounces) crushed tomatoes
- 1 cup vegetable broth
- 1/8 teaspoon crushed red pepper flakes
- 8 ounces uncooked ziti *or* small tube pasta
- 1 cup (8 ounces) part-skim ricotta cheese
- 1/2 cup shredded provolone cheese
- 1/4 cup loosely packed basil leaves, thinly sliced
- 1 cup (4 ounces) shredded part-skim mozzarella cheese
- 1/4 cup grated Parmesan cheese

1 In a large nonstick skillet coated with cooking spray, saute the onion, green pepper and carrots until crisp-tender. Add garlic; cook 1 minute longer. Stir in the tomatoes, broth and pepper flakes; bring to a boil. Reduce heat; simmer, uncovered, for 15 minutes.

2 Meanwhile, cook ziti according to package directions; drain and return to pan. Stir in the vegetable mixture, ricotta cheese, provolone cheese and basil.

3 Transfer to a 13-in. x 9-in. baking dish coated with cooking spray. Sprinkle with mozzarella cheese and Parmesan cheese. Bake, uncovered, at 425° for 10-15 minutes or until heated through and cheese is melted.

YIELD: 8 SERVINGS.

tuna veggie macaroni

Al Robbins, Chandler, Arizona

After much experimenting with various versions, it all boiled down to this one super-delicious recipe. My family can't get enough of it.

1-1/4 cups uncooked elbow macaroni
5 ounces process cheese (Velveeta), cubed
1/2 cup milk
2 cups frozen peas and carrots, thawed
1 can (5 ounces) white water-packed tuna, drained
1/4 teaspoon dill weed

1 Cook the macaroni according to package directions; drain. Add cheese and milk; stir until cheese is melted. Stir in the vegetables, tuna and dill; heat through.

YIELD: 3 SERVINGS.

farmhouse chili dogs

Catherine Braley, Barboursville, West Virginia

We host lots of hay rides, picnics, hot dog roasts and ice cream socials on our farm, and these chili dogs never fail to please. There's always someone who fills a cup with the sauce and eats it straight.

1 pound ground beef
1 medium onion, chopped
1 can (10-3/4 ounces) condensed tomato soup, undiluted
1/2 cup water
3 tablespoons ketchup
1 tablespoon sugar

1-1/2 teaspoons chili powder
8 hot dogs
8 hot dog buns, split
Shredded cheddar cheese, optional

1 In a large skillet, cook beef and onion over medium heat until meat is no longer pink; drain. Stir in the soup, water, ketchup, sugar and chili powder; bring to a boil. Reduce heat; simmer, uncovered, for 20 minutes or until thickened.

2 Cook hot dogs according to package directions. Place in buns; top with meat sauce. Sprinkle with cheese if desired.

YIELD: 8 SERVINGS.

crunchy ham and cheese

(pictured at right)

Karen Wolf, Niles, Illinois

Crushed potato chips put the crunch in this appetizing variation on ham and cheese. Serve this layered sandwich with a bowl of soup, and you'll have one of the best comfort-food meals of your life.

1 tablespoon butter, softened
4 slices white bread
1 tablespoon Dijon mustard
4 slices process American cheese
2 slices deli ham (1 ounce *each*)
1/2 medium tomato, thinly sliced
2 eggs
2 tablespoons 2% milk
1/8 teaspoon onion powder
1 cup crushed ridged potato chips

1 Butter one side of each slice of bread. Spread mustard over the unbuttered side of two slices; layer each with one slice of cheese, ham, tomato, remaining cheese and remaining bread, buttered side up.

2 In a shallow bowl, whisk the eggs, milk and onion powder. Place potato chips in another bowl. Dip each sandwich into egg mixture, then coat with potato chips.

3 In a large nonstick skillet coated with cooking spray, toast sandwiches for 4 minutes on each side or until golden brown.

YIELD: 2 SERVINGS.

southwest tortilla pizzas

(pictured at left)

Martha Pollock, Oregonia, Ohio

Here's a colorful and filling meal that couldn't be much simpler to prepare on busy weeknights. Kids will have fun as they help you put these together.

- 1 can (16 ounces) refried beans
- 1 can (4 ounces) chopped green chilies, drained
- 1/4 teaspoon garlic powder
- 1/4 teaspoon ground cumin
- 1/4 teaspoon chili powder
- 8 flour tortillas (6 inches)
- 3/4 cup salsa
- 1/2 cup chopped green pepper
- 1/2 cup chopped sweet onion
- 3/4 cup shredded cheddar cheese

1 In a small bowl, combine the first five ingredients. Place four tortillas on an ungreased baking sheet; spread with bean mixture to within 1/2 in. of the edges. Top with remaining tortillas. Spoon salsa over tops. Sprinkle with pepper, onion and cheese.

2 Bake at 400° for 10-15 minutes or until cheese is melted.

YIELD: 4 SERVINGS.

fruited coleslaw

Linda Stevens, Madison, Alabama

We all need to get more fruits and vegetables into our diets, and this dish is a great-tasting way to do it.

2 cups coleslaw mix
1 snack-size cup (4 ounces) mandarin oranges, drained
1/2 cup chopped apple
1/4 cup mayonnaise
2 teaspoons honey
1/4 teaspoon poppy seeds

1 In a small bowl, combine the coleslaw mix, oranges and apple. Combine the remaining ingredients; pour over coleslaw mixture and toss to coat. Cover and refrigerate for at least 2 hours before serving.

YIELD: 3 SERVINGS.

pork barbecue sandwiches

George Hascher, Phoenicia, New York

Growing up, we were happy to see pork roast on the menu because we were sure that, within the next few days, we'd be feasting on leftover pork in these tasty sandwiches.

- 2 celery ribs, finely chopped
- 1 medium onion, finely chopped
- 1 teaspoon canola oil
- 1 cup ketchup
- 1 to 1-1/2 teaspoons salt
- 1 teaspoon ground mustard
- 2 cups shredded cooked pork
- 2 to 3 kaiser rolls *or* hamburger buns, split

1 In a large saucepan, saute celery and onion in oil until tender. Stir in the ketchup, salt and mustard. Add pork. Bring to a boil. Reduce heat; cover and simmer for 20-30 minutes to allow flavors to blend. Serve on rolls.

YIELD: 2-3 SERVINGS.

barbecue chicken pita pizzas

Staca Hiatt, Twentynine Palms, California

I use bottled barbecue sauce, cooked chicken breast, and cheddar cheese for a truly Western-style pizza. These are very easy to prepare.

- 1 cup finely chopped cooked chicken
- 1/2 cup barbecue sauce
- 4 pita breads (6 inches)
- 1/3 cup real bacon bits
- 1 small onion, halved and thinly sliced
- 1 small green pepper, julienned
- 1 can (4 ounces) chopped green chilies
- 1 can (4 ounces) mushroom stems and pieces, drained
- 1 cup (4 ounces) shredded cheddar cheese

1 In a small bowl, combine chicken and barbecue sauce; spoon over pitas. Top with the bacon, onion, pepper, chilies, mushrooms and cheese.

2 Place on an ungreased baking sheet. Bake at 450° for 8-10 minutes or until heated through.

YIELD: 4 SERVINGS.

ham mac and cheese

Susan Taul, Birmingham, Alabama

I've been using this classic recipe for years. It's perfect with a salad for dinner and is popular at potlucks.

- 1 package (7-1/4 ounces) macaroni and cheese dinner mix
- 3/4 cup soft bread crumbs
- 2 tablespoons grated Parmesan cheese
- 1 tablespoon minced fresh parsley
- 1 tablespoon butter, melted
- 1 cup cubed fully cooked ham
- 1 cup (8 ounces) cream-style cottage cheese
- 1/2 cup sour cream
- 2 tablespoons sliced green onion
- 1 tablespoon diced pimientos, optional
- 1/4 teaspoon salt
- 1/4 teaspoon ground mustard

1 Prepare macaroni and cheese according to package directions. Meanwhile, in a small bowl, combine the bread crumbs, Parmesan cheese, parsley and butter; set aside.

2 In a large bowl, combine macaroni and cheese, ham, cottage cheese, sour cream, onion, pimientos if desired, salt and mustard. Place in a greased 1-1/2 qt. baking dish. Sprinkle with crumb mixture. Bake, uncovered, at 350° for 35-40 minutes or until heated through.

YIELD: 4 SERVINGS.

chili sausage supper

Phillis Moore, Excelsior Springs, Missouri

The pork sausage in this one-skillet dish offers plenty of flavor, and the chili powder adds a little kick. It's a nice supper that's a snap to make.

1/2	pound bulk pork sausage
1/3	cup finely chopped onion
1/3	cup chopped green pepper
2	cups uncooked egg noodles
1	cup canned diced tomatoes
3/4	cup water
1-1/2	teaspoons sugar
1/2	teaspoon chili powder
1/4	teaspoon salt, optional
1/2	cup sour cream

1 In a large skillet, cook the sausage, onion and green pepper over medium heat until meat is no longer pink; drain. Stir in the noodles, tomatoes, water, sugar, chili powder and salt if desired. Bring to a boil. Reduce heat; cover and simmer for 30 minutes or until noodles are tender.

2 Gradually stir 1/2 cup hot sausage mixture into sour cream; return all to the pan, stirring constantly. Cook until heated through.

YIELD: 2 SERVINGS.

kid-sized classic pizza

(pictured at left)

Taste of Home Test Kitchen

This downsized pizza tastes just as good as its bigger counterpart. Frozen dinner rolls make a time-saving crust that still provides delicious, from-scratch flavor. Your child can help roll out the dough, spread the sauce and sprinkle on the toppings.

1   Italian sausage link (1/4 pound), casing removed
2   frozen bread dough dinner rolls, thawed
1/4   cup pizza sauce
1/2   cup shredded part-skim mozzarella cheese
5   slices pepperoni
1/2   teaspoon Italian seasoning

1 Crumble sausage into a small skillet. Cook over medium heat until no longer pink; drain. On a lightly floured surface, knead the dinner rolls together. Roll dough into a 7-1/2-in. circle. Transfer to a greased pizza pan or baking sheet.

2 Spread with pizza sauce; sprinkle with 1/4 cup cheese. Top with sausage, pepperoni, Italian seasoning and remaining cheese. Bake at 375° for 20-22 minutes or until crust is golden brown.

YIELD: 1 SERVING.

sausage mostaccioli

Janet Roehring, Marble Falls, Texas

This comforting pasta dish is always a star with my family. It smells wonderful when baking in the oven.

1 pound Italian sausage links, sliced
1 jar (15 ounces) spaghetti sauce
8 ounces mostaccioli, cooked and drained
1/3 cup grated Parmesan cheese
1 cup (4 ounces) shredded part-skim mozzarella cheese

1 In a large skillet, cook sausage over medium heat until no longer pink; drain. In a greased 2-qt. baking dish, combine the sausage, sauce, mostaccioli and Parmesan cheese. Top with mozzarella cheese.

2 Bake, uncovered, at 350° for 15-20 minutes or until heated through.

YIELD: 4-6 SERVINGS.

bacon cheeseburger roll-ups

Jessica Cain, Des Moines, Iowa

My husband and I both love these fun roll-ups. They must be good, because this recipe won a first place prize at the Iowa State Fair!

1   pound ground beef
6   bacon strips, diced
1/2   cup chopped onion
1   package (8 ounces) process cheese (Velveeta), cubed
1   tube (16.3 ounces) large refrigerated buttermilk biscuits
1/2   cup ketchup
1/4   cup yellow mustard

1 In a large skillet, cook the beef, bacon and onion over medium heat until meat is no longer pink; drain. Add cheese; cook and stir until melted. Remove from the heat.

2 Flatten each biscuit into a 5-in. circle; spoon 1/3 cup beef mixture onto each biscuit. Fold sides and ends over filling and roll up. Place seam side down on a greased baking sheet.

3 Bake at 400° for 18-20 minutes or until golden brown. In a small bowl, combine ketchup and mustard; serve with roll-ups.

YIELD: 8 ROLL-UPS.

kielbasa biscuit pizza

Jennifer Zukiwsky, Glendon, Alberta

My family enjoys this extremely quick and very tasty pizza. It's a bit different because you use buttermilk biscuits instead of pizza dough. It makes enough for a large family and is great for company.

    2   tubes (12 ounces *each*) refrigerated buttermilk
         biscuits
2-1/2 cups garden-style spaghetti sauce
  1/2   pound smoked kielbasa *or* Polish sausage, cubed
    1   can (8 ounces) mushroom stems and pieces, drained
  1/2   cup chopped green pepper
  1/2   cup chopped sweet red pepper
    1   cup (4 ounces) shredded part-skim mozzarella cheese
    1   cup (4 ounces) shredded cheddar cheese

1 Separate biscuits; cut each biscuit into fourths. Arrange in a greased 13-in. x 9-in. baking dish (do not flatten). Bake at 375° for 12-15 minutes or until biscuits begin to brown.

2 Spread spaghetti sauce over biscuit crust. Sprinkle with the sausage, mushrooms, peppers and cheeses. Bake for 20-25 minutes or until bubbly and cheese is melted. Let stand for 5 minutes before cutting.

YIELD: 8 SERVINGS.

pizza spaghetti

Robert Smith, Las Vegas, Nevada

The idea for this recipe came to me when I saw someone dip a slice of pizza into a pasta dish. My wife and kids love it and so do my friends!

  1/2   pound lean ground beef (90% lean)
  1/2   pound Italian turkey sausage links, casings
         removed, crumbled
  1/2   cup chopped sweet onion
    4   cans (8 ounces *each*) no-salt-added tomato sauce
    3   ounces sliced turkey pepperoni
    1   tablespoon sugar
    2   teaspoons minced fresh parsley *or* 1/2 teaspoon
         dried parsley flakes
    2   teaspoons minced fresh basil *or* 1/2 teaspoon
         dried basil
    9   ounces uncooked whole wheat spaghetti
    3   tablespoons grated Parmesan cheese

1 In a large nonstick skillet, cook the beef, sausage and onion over medium heat until meat is no longer pink; drain.

2 Stir in the tomato sauce, pepperoni, sugar, parsley and basil. Bring to a boil. Reduce heat; simmer, uncovered, for 20-25 minutes or until sauce is thickened. Meanwhile, cook spaghetti according to package directions.

3 Drain spaghetti; toss with sauce. Sprinkle with Parmesan cheese.

YIELD: 6 SERVINGS.

tacos in a bowl

Sue Schoening, Sheboygan, Wisconsin

Here's a wonderful, oh-so-easy dish that young people adore. If you have leftover taco meat, kids can really whip this up quickly. Garnish each serving with sour cream and salsa for a little more Southwestern flair.

1/2 pound lean ground beef (90% lean)
2 tablespoons finely chopped onion
3/4 cup canned diced tomatoes, drained
2 tablespoons taco seasoning
1 cup water
1 package (3 ounces) ramen noodles
1/4 cup shredded cheddar *or* Mexican cheese blend
1/4 cup crushed tortilla chips, optional

1 In a small skillet, cook beef and onion over medium heat until meat is no longer pink; drain. Stir in the tomatoes, taco seasoning and water. Bring to a boil. Add ramen noodles (discard seasoning packet or save for another use). Cook and stir for 3-5 minutes or until noodles are tender.

2 Spoon into serving bowls; sprinkle with cheese and tortilla chips if desired.

YIELD: 2 SERVINGS.

alfredo chicken tortellini

(pictured at left)

Tiffany Treanor, Waukomis, Oklahoma

I'm always trying to come up with something new, and for this recipe, I just started putting things together. This is so rich and creamy, it's a keeper.

1-1/2 cups frozen cheese tortellini
1 boneless skinless chicken breast half (6 ounces), cut into 1-inch cubes
3 bacon strips, chopped
1/8 teaspoon adobo seasoning
1/3 cup chopped onion
1/3 cup chopped sweet red pepper
3 teaspoons minced garlic
1 can (10-3/4 ounces) condensed cream of chicken soup, undiluted
1/2 cup 2% milk
1/3 cup sour cream
2 tablespoons grated Parmesan cheese
1 cup frozen chopped broccoli, thawed and drained

1 Cook tortellini according to package directions. Meanwhile, in a large saucepan, cook and stir the chicken, bacon and adobo seasoning over medium heat until chicken is no longer pink. Add onion and red pepper; cook and stir until tender. Add garlic; cook 1 minute longer.

2 In a small bowl, combine the soup, milk, sour cream and Parmesan cheese; stir into chicken mixture. Bring to a boil. Reduce heat; simmer, uncovered, for 5-7 minutes.

3 Drain tortellini; add to chicken mixture. Stir in broccoli; heat through.

YIELD: 3 SERVINGS.

ham 'n' cheese pasta

Karen Kopp, Indianapolis, Indiana

My mother would prepare this yummy comfort food whenever there was leftover ham. Horseradish gives it a nice tangy taste. I quickened the preparation by using process cheese instead of making a cheese sauce from scratch. My kids love it, too.

8 ounces uncooked medium pasta shells
1 pound process cheese (Velveeta), cubed
1/2 cup milk
2 tablespoons ketchup
1 tablespoon prepared horseradish
2 cups cubed fully cooked ham
1 package (8 ounces) frozen peas, thawed

1 Cook pasta according to package directions. Meanwhile, in a microwave-safe bowl, combine cheese and milk. Cover and microwave on high for 2 minutes; stir. Heat 1-2 minutes longer or until smooth, stirring twice. Stir in ketchup and horseradish until blended.

2 Drain pasta and place in a large bowl. Stir in the ham, peas and cheese sauce.

3 Transfer to a greased 2-qt. baking dish. Cover and bake at 350° for 30-35 minutes or until bubbly.

YIELD: 4 SERVINGS.

EDITOR'S NOTE: This recipe was tested in a 1,100-watt microwave.

catalina taco salad

(pictured at right)

Kay Curtis, Guthrie, Oklahoma

This quick taco salad is popular with the teen campers at the youth camp my husband directs. Our daughter has requested it 2 years in a row for her birthday dinner.

1-1/2 pounds lean ground beef (90% lean)
   3 cups (12 ounces) shredded cheddar cheese
   1 can (15 ounces) pinto beans, rinsed and drained
   2 medium tomatoes, seeded and chopped
   1 large onion, chopped
   1 bunch romaine, torn
   1 package (12 ounces) corn chips
   1 bottle (24 ounces) Catalina salad dressing

1 In a large skillet, cook beef over medium heat until no longer pink; drain.

2 Transfer to a large serving bowl. Add the cheese, beans, tomatoes, onion, romaine and corn chips. Drizzle with dressing; gently toss to coat.

YIELD: 12 SERVINGS.

chili mac skillet

Tracy Golder, Bloomsburg, Pennsylvania

Speedy stovetop preparation and zippy flavor make this dish a dinnertime winner. Both children and adults give it a thumbs-up.

1-1/4 cups uncooked elbow macaroni
   1 pound ground beef
   1 medium onion, chopped
   1 medium green pepper, chopped
   2 garlic cloves, minced
   2 cans (14-1/2 ounces *each*) diced tomatoes, undrained
   1 can (16 ounces) kidney beans, rinsed and drained
   1 package (10 ounces) frozen corn, thawed
   2 tablespoons chili powder
1/2 to 1 teaspoon salt
1/2 teaspoon ground cumin
1/2 cup shredded pepper Jack cheese

1 Cook macaroni according to package directions. Meanwhile, in a large skillet, cook the beef, onion and green pepper over medium heat until meat is no longer pink and vegetables are tender. Add garlic; cook 1 minute longer. Drain.

2 Stir in the tomatoes, beans, corn, chili powder, salt and cumin. Bring to a boil. Reduce heat; cover and simmer for 15 minutes.

3 Drain the macaroni and add to skillet; stir to coat. Sprinkle with cheese.

YIELD: 8 SERVINGS.

parmesan peas 'n' rice

Inge Schermerhorn, Kingston, New Hampshire

Here is a wonderful complement to any meal. My husband likes rice but isn't crazy about peas, and I'm just the opposite. This is a great compromise!

1/3 cup uncooked long grain rice
   1 green onion, chopped
   1 tablespoon butter
   1 cup chicken broth
1/8 teaspoon pepper
2/3 cup frozen peas, thawed
   1 tablespoon grated Parmesan cheese

1 In a small saucepan, saute rice and onion in butter until onion is tender. Stir in broth and pepper. Bring to a boil. Reduce heat; cover and simmer for 10 minutes.

2 Add peas; cover and cook 5-6 minutes longer or until liquid is absorbed and rice is tender. Stir in cheese.

YIELD: 2 SERVINGS.

double-cheese ziti with bacon

Taste of Home Test Kitchen

This mac and cheese is real comfort food. No one can resist the combination of cheesy pasta, golden bread crumbs and bacon!

1   package (16 ounces) ziti *or* small tube pasta
3   cups (24 ounces) 4% cottage cheese
1/2   cup plus 1 tablespoon butter, *divided*
1/2   cup all-purpose flour
1   teaspoon salt
1/2   teaspoon white pepper
1/4   teaspoon garlic salt
3   cups half-and-half cream
1   cup milk
4   cups (16 ounces) shredded cheddar cheese
1   cup crumbled cooked bacon, *divided*
1/3   cup dry bread crumbs

1   Cook pasta according to package directions. Meanwhile, place cottage cheese in a food processor; cover and process until smooth. Set cottage cheese aside.

2   In a large saucepan, melt 1/2 cup butter. Stir in the flour, salt, pepper and garlic salt until smooth. Gradually add cream and milk. Bring to a boil; cook and stir for 2 minutes or until thickened.

3   Drain macaroni; transfer to a large bowl. Add the cheddar cheese, cottage cheese, white sauce and 3/4 cup bacon; toss to coat. Transfer to a greased 13-in. x 9-in. baking dish. (Dish will be full.) Melt remaining butter. Add bread crumbs; toss to coat. Sprinkle over casserole.

4   Bake, uncovered, at 400° for 20 minutes. Sprinkle with remaining bacon. Bake 5 minutes longer or until bubbly.

YIELD: 12 SERVINGS (1 CUP EACH).

homemade fish sticks

Jennifer Rowland, Elizabethtown, Kentucky

I'm a nutritionist, and I needed a healthy fish fix. Moist on the inside and crunchy on the outside, these are great with oven fries or roasted veggies and low-fat homemade tartar sauce.

1/2 cup all-purpose flour
 1   egg, beaten
1/2 cup dry bread crumbs
1/2 teaspoon salt
1/2 teaspoon paprika
1/2 teaspoon lemon-pepper seasoning
3/4 pound cod fillets, cut into 1-inch strips
Butter-flavored cooking spray

1 Place flour and egg in separate shallow bowls. In another shallow bowl, combine bread crumbs and seasonings. Dip fish in the flour, then egg, then roll in the crumb mixture.

2 Place on a baking sheet coated with cooking spray. Spritz fish sticks with butter-flavored spray. Bake at 400° for 5-6 minutes on each side or until fish flakes easily with a fork.

YIELD: 2 SERVINGS.

chicken salad shells

Karen Lee, Waynesville, North Carolina

These stuffed shells are great for a cool summer meal. Calling for just four ingredients, including chicken salad from the deli, they're so fast to assemble.

1-1/2 pounds prepared chicken salad
1/2 cup seedless red grapes, halved
18 jumbo pasta shells, cooked, drained and cooled
2/3 cup ranch salad dressing

1 In a large bowl, combine the chicken salad and grapes. Spoon about 2 tablespoons into each pasta shell. Refrigerate until serving. Drizzle with salad dressing.

YIELD: 6 SERVINGS.

cheeseburger cups

(pictured at right)

Jeri Millhouse, Ashland, Ohio

A terrific recipe for parents with young children and busy lives, this simple dish takes just a short time. Best of all, kids will go absolutely crazy for these adorable dinner bites!

- 1 pound ground beef
- 1/2 cup ketchup
- 2 tablespoons brown sugar
- 1 tablespoon prepared mustard
- 1-1/2 teaspoons Worcestershire sauce
- 1 tube (12 ounces) refrigerated buttermilk biscuits
- 1/2 cup cubed process cheese (Velveeta)

1 In a large skillet, cook beef over medium heat until no longer pink; drain. Stir in the ketchup, brown sugar, mustard and Worcestershire sauce. Remove from the heat; set aside.

2 Press each biscuit onto the bottom and up the sides of a greased muffin cup. Spoon beef mixture into cups; top with cheese cubes. Bake at 400° for 14-16 minutes or until golden brown.

YIELD: 10 CHEESEBURGER CUPS.

taco macaroni

Elizabeth King, Duluth, Minnesota

Comforting mac and cheese with a touch of taco flavoring and tortilla-chip crunch—no wonder kids love it! Moms will love that it's ready in no time flat and isn't expensive to make.

- 2 packages (7-1/4 ounces each) macaroni and cheese dinner mix
- 1 pound ground beef
- 1 cup chunky salsa
- 2 cups crushed tortilla chips
- 1 can (2-1/4 ounces) sliced ripe olives, drained
- 2 cups (8 ounces each) shredded Mexican cheese blend

Sour cream, optional

1 Prepare macaroni and cheese according to package directions. Meanwhile, in a large skillet, cook beef until no longer pink; drain. Stir in salsa; set aside.

2 Spread macaroni into a greased 13-in. x 9-in. baking dish. Layer with beef mixture, chips and olives; sprinkle with cheese.

3 Bake, uncovered, at 350° for 15-20 minutes or until heated through. Serve with sour cream if desired.

YIELD: 8 SERVINGS.

chili biscuit bake

Sara Martin, Whitefish, Montana

Your whole gang will enjoy this zesty Mexican bake. It's a tasty new take on tacos.

- 1 pound lean ground beef (90% lean)
- 2/3 cup water
- 1 envelope taco seasoning
- 2 tubes (12 ounces each) refrigerated buttermilk biscuits
- 1 can (15 ounces) chili con carne
- 1 cup (4 ounces) shredded reduced-fat cheddar cheese

Salsa and sour cream, optional

1 In a large skillet, cook beef until no longer pink; drain. Stir in water and taco seasoning. Bring to a boil; cook and stir for 2 minutes or until thickened.

2 Meanwhile, quarter biscuits; place in a greased 13-in. x 9-in. baking dish. Layer with beef mixture, chili and cheese. Bake, uncovered, at 375° for 25-30 minutes or until cheese is melted and biscuits are golden brown. Serve with salsa and sour cream if desired.

YIELD: 8 SERVINGS.

cola barbecue ribs

(pictured at left)

Karen Shuck, Edgar, Nebraska

Enjoy the smoky goodness of a summer barbecue all year long by preparing these ribs in your slow cooker.

1/4 cup packed brown sugar
2 garlic cloves, minced
1 teaspoon salt
1/2 teaspoon pepper
3 tablespoons Liquid Smoke, optional
4 pounds pork spareribs, cut into serving-size pieces
1 medium onion, sliced
1/2 cup cola
1-1/2 cups barbecue sauce

1 In a small bowl, combine the brown sugar, garlic, salt, pepper and Liquid Smoke if desired; rub over ribs.

2 Layer ribs and onion in a greased 5- or 6-qt. slow cooker; pour cola over ribs. Cover and cook on low for 8-10 hours or until ribs are tender. Drain liquid. Pour sauce over ribs and cook 1 hour longer.

YIELD: 4 SERVINGS.

honey mustard pork

Janet Les, Chilliwack, British Columbia

Dijon mustard and honey create a sweet and subtly tangy sauce that perfectly complements lean pork tenderloin.

1 pound pork tenderloin, cut into thin strips
1 tablespoon canola oil
1 cup reduced-sodium beef broth, *divided*
1/4 cup honey
1 tablespoon Dijon mustard
1 tablespoon cornstarch
2 tablespoons cold water
Hot cooked long grain and wild rice, optional

1 In a large nonstick skillet, brown pork in oil. Add 1/2 cup broth. Bring to a boil. Reduce heat; cover and simmer 10 minutes or until meat is no longer pink. Remove pork with a slotted spoon and keep warm.

2 Stir in the honey, mustard and remaining broth. Combine cornstarch and water until smooth. Gradually stir into the pan. Bring to a boil; cook and stir for 2 minutes or until thickened. Return pork to the pan; heat through. Serve with rice if desired.

YIELD: 4 SERVINGS.

kid-pleasing taco pizza

Kimberly Theobald, Galesburg, Illinois

Kids will love this quick and easy take on both tacos and pizza. And you'll love that it's full of flavor and lower in fat and calories!

1 tube (13.8 ounces) refrigerated pizza crust
1 pound lean ground turkey
3/4 cup water
1 envelope reduced-sodium taco seasoning
1 can (16 ounces) fat-free refried beans
1-1/2 cups (6 ounces) shredded pizza cheese blend
3 medium tomatoes, chopped
7 cups shredded lettuce
2 cups crushed baked tortilla chip scoops

1 Unroll crust into a 15-in. x 10-in. x 1-in. baking pan coated with cooking spray; flatten dough and build up edges slightly. Bake at 425° for 8-10 minutes or until edges are lightly browned.

2 Meanwhile, in a large nonstick skillet, cook turkey over medium heat until no longer pink; drain. Stir in water and taco seasoning. Bring to a boil. Reduce heat; simmer, uncovered, for 5 minutes. Stir in refried beans until blended.

3 Spread turkey mixture over crust; sprinkle with cheese. Bake at 425° for 5-7 minutes or until cheese is melted. Top with tomatoes, lettuce and chips. Serve immediately.

YIELD: 10 PIECES.

1/4 cup butter, melted
2 tablespoons lemon juice
1 package (11.4 ounces) frozen breaded fish sticks
2 tablespoons mayonnaise
6 hot dog buns, split
Shredded lettuce, chopped onion and
    chopped tomatoes, optional

1 In a shallow bowl, combine butter and lemon juice. Dip fish sticks in butter mixture. Place in a single layer in an ungreased baking pan. Bake at 400° for 15-18 minutes or until crispy.

2 Spread mayonnaise on bun bottoms; add fish sticks. Top with lettuce, onion and tomato if desired. Replace bun tops.

YIELD: 6 SERVINGS.

confetti rice

Lora Billmire, Spokane, Washington

Dried cranberries lend a splash of color to this appealing recipe. I think it makes a great side dish for Thanksgiving or Christmas.

2 tablespoons chopped onion
2 tablespoons chopped celery
2 teaspoons canola oil
2/3 cup chicken broth
1/3 cup uncooked long grain rice
1/4 teaspoon salt
Dash pepper
2 tablespoons slivered almonds
2 tablespoons dried cranberries

1 In a small saucepan, saute onion and celery in oil until tender. Add the broth, rice, salt and pepper. Bring to a boil, stirring occasionally. Reduce heat; cover and simmer for 10 minutes. Add almonds and cranberries.

2 Cover and simmer 9-11 minutes longer or until rice is tender. Fluff with a fork. Serve warm.

YIELD: 2 SERVINGS.

fish stick sandwiches

Cherie Durbin, Hickory, North Carolina

Make the most of convenient frozen fish sticks with these fun, family-pleasing sandwiches. My mom made these whenever she wanted fish in a hurry.

hearty pizza casserole

(pictured at right)

Barbara Walker, Brookville, Kansas

This cheesy, meaty meal is easy to make and can be prepared ahead of time. I decreased the recipe size so we can enjoy it more often.

1 cup uncooked elbow macaroni
1/2 pound lean ground beef (90% lean)
6 small fresh mushrooms, halved
1/3 cup chopped onion
1 can (8 ounces) tomato sauce
1 package (3-1/2 ounces) sliced pepperoni
2 tablespoons sliced ripe olives
1 teaspoon sugar
3/4 teaspoon Italian seasoning
1/4 teaspoon pepper
1/4 cup shredded cheddar cheese
1/4 cup shredded part-skim mozzarella cheese

1 Cook macaroni according to package directions. Meanwhile, in a large skillet, cook the beef, mushrooms and onion over medium heat until meat is no longer pink; drain. Stir in the tomato sauce, pepperoni, olives, sugar, Italian seasoning and pepper.

2 Drain macaroni; add to meat mixture. Transfer to a 1-1/2-qt. baking dish coated with cooking spray. Sprinkle with cheeses. Bake, uncovered, at 350° for 20-25 minutes or until heated through.

YIELD: 4 SERVINGS.

pizza parlor pasta

Shelley Pimlott, Nashua, Iowa

I usually serve this cheesy main course with slices of garlic bread. It reminds me of a pasta specialty at our favorite pizza place.

- 1 cup uncooked medium pasta shells
- 1/3 pound bulk Italian sausage
- 1/2 small onion, finely chopped
- 3 tablespoons finely chopped green pepper
- 1-1/3 cups spaghetti sauce
- 1/3 cup 1% cottage cheese
- 1/2 cup shredded part-skim mozzarella cheese, *divided*
- 1/2 cup shredded Colby-Monterey Jack cheese, *divided*
- 2 tablespoons grated Parmesan cheese

1 Cook pasta according to package directions. Meanwhile, crumble the sausage into a small skillet; add onion and green pepper. Cook over medium heat until meat is no longer pink. Stir in the spaghetti sauce, cottage cheese, 1/4 cup mozzarella cheese and 1/4 cup Colby-Monterey Jack cheese.

2 Drain pasta; stir into sausage mixture. Transfer to a 1-qt. baking dish coated with cooking spray. Sprinkle with remaining shredded cheeses. Top with Parmesan cheese.

3 Bake, uncovered, at 350° for 5-10 minutes or until cheese is melted.

YIELD: 3 SERVINGS.

meatball sandwiches

Ruby Steigleder, Selma, California

These crowd-pleasing sandwiches are great when you're hosting a holiday open house or progressive dinner. Keep the meatballs warm in a slow cooker on your buffet table, and guests can serve themselves as they arrive.

- 1 egg, lightly beaten
- 1/2 cup milk
- 1/2 cup dry bread crumbs
- 1/4 cup finely chopped onion
- 1/2 teaspoon salt
- 1/4 teaspoon garlic powder
- 1/4 teaspoon pepper
- 1-1/2 pounds ground beef

BARBECUE SAUCE:
- 1 large onion, chopped
- 2 tablespoons canola oil
- 2 garlic cloves, minced
- 3 cups water
- 1 can (12 ounces) tomato paste
- 2 teaspoons salt
- 1 teaspoon sugar
- 1 teaspoon dried oregano
- 1/4 teaspoon pepper
- 1 bay leaf
- 14 submarine buns (6 inches *each*), split
- 1-3/4 cups shredded part-skim mozzarella cheese

1 In a large bowl, combine the egg, milk, bread crumbs, onion, salt, garlic powder and pepper. Crumble beef over mixture and mix well. Shape into 1-1/2-in. balls. Place on a greased rack in a shallow baking pan. Bake, uncovered, at 350° for 30-35 minutes or until no longer pink. Drain on paper towels.

2 Meanwhile, for sauce, in a Dutch oven, saute onion in oil for 3-4 minutes or until tender. Add garlic; cook 1 minute longer. Stir in the water, tomato paste, salt, sugar, oregano, pepper and bay leaf. Bring to a boil. Add the meatballs. Reduce heat; simmer, uncovered, for 10-15 minutes or until heated through.

3 Discard bay leaf. Spoon meatballs with sauce onto bun bottoms. Sprinkle with cheese. Replace the bun tops.

YIELD: 14 SERVINGS.

hash browns with ham

Lightningbug, Taste of Home Online Community

Convenient grocery store items like frozen hash browns and a can of chicken soup make this an easy-to-prepare dish. Both kids and adults love it because it's tasty and chock-full of cheese.

- 1 package (32 ounces) frozen cubed hash brown potatoes, thawed
- 1 cup cubed fully cooked ham
- 1 small onion, chopped
- 2 cups (8 ounces) shredded cheddar cheese, *divided*
- 1 can (14-3/4 ounces) condensed cream of chicken soup, undiluted
- 1/2 cup butter, melted
- 1 cup (8 ounces) sour cream

1 In a 3-qt. slow cooker, combine the potatoes, ham, onion and 1 cup cheese. Combine soup and butter; pour over potato mixture. Cover and cook on low for 3-4 hours or until potatoes are tender.

2 Stir in the sour cream. Sprinkle with remaining cheese. Cover and cook for 15 minutes or until cheese is melted.

YIELD: 8 SERVINGS.

crunchy
munchies

abc cheese dip

Kimberly Miller, Norfolk, Virginia

Both the young and young at heart will dig right into this delightfully seasoned dip. It isn't too garlicky, so kids will like it. For a fun after-school treat, try cutting the carrots and peppers with alphabet- and numeral-shaped cookie cutters to serve as dippers.

- 1 package (8 ounces) cream cheese, softened
- 2 tablespoons milk
- 1/2 to 1 teaspoon garlic salt
- 2 tablespoons *each* chopped green, sweet red and yellow pepper

Carrots and additional peppers
Alphabet cookie cutters (about 1 inch)
Numeral cookie cutters (about 1-1/2 inches)

1 In a large bowl, beat the cream cheese, milk and garlic salt until smooth. Stir in chopped peppers. Cut carrots and peppers into letters and numbers; serve with dip.

YIELD: 1 CUP.

creepy-crawly bugs

Taste of Home Test Kitchen

Who wouldn't want to eat our cute little bugs? Quick and easy prep and undeniable kid appeal make these a must-have for the buffet at a child's party.

- 1 tube (11 ounces) refrigerated breadsticks
- 8 smoked sausage links *or* hot dogs
- 1/2 to 3/4 cup potato sticks

Ketchup *and/or* mustard

1 Separate dough into strips. Unroll and cut eight strips in half widthwise; set remaining strips aside. Cut sausages in half widthwise. Wrap one piece of dough around each sausage, leaving the rounded end showing. Place seam side down on an ungreased baking sheet. Place reserved breadsticks on baking sheet.

2 Bake at 350° for 15-17 minutes or until golden brown. Remove bugs to a serving plate and cool for 2 minutes.

3 Insert potato sticks into baked dough to resemble legs and antennae. Decorate with ketchup and/or mustard. Serve warm. Save remaining breadsticks for another use.

YIELD: 8 SERVINGS.

EDITOR'S NOTE: Refrigerated crescent rolls may be used in place of the breadsticks. Follow package directions for baking temperature and time.

pizza egg rolls

(pictured at left)

Tammy Schill, Omaha, Nebraska

My husband and kids love these very untraditional egg rolls. Their crispy wrappers and flavorful pizza filling make them taste so good!

1   pound bulk Italian sausage
3/4   cup diced green pepper
1   garlic clove, minced
1   can (15 ounces) crushed tomatoes
1/4   cup tomato paste
1/2   teaspoon salt
1/2   teaspoon dried oregano
1/4   teaspoon sugar
1/8   teaspoon dried rosemary, crushed
Dash pepper
8   ounces cubed part-skim mozzarella cheese
13   egg roll wrappers
1   egg, lightly beaten
Oil for frying

1 In a large skillet, cook sausage and green pepper over medium heat until meat is no longer pink. Add garlic; cook 1 minute longer. Drain. Stir in the tomatoes, tomato paste and seasonings. Bring to a boil. Reduce heat; cover and simmer for 10 minutes. Uncover and simmer 10 minutes longer. Remove from the heat; cool for 20 minutes. Stir in cheese.

2 Place 1/3 cup sausage mixture in the center of each egg roll wrapper. Fold bottom corner over filling; fold sides toward center over filling. Brush remaining corner with egg; roll up tightly to seal.

3 In an electric skillet or deep-fat fryer, heat 1 in. of oil to 375°. Fry egg rolls in batches for 1-2 minutes on each side or until golden brown. Drain on paper towels.

YIELD: 13 EGG ROLLS.

mini veggie wagon

Nella Parker, Hersey, Michigan

I received a lot of compliments on these wagons at our family reunion. Even the youngsters had a fun time eating their vegetables right down to the cucumber wagon wheels!

2   celery ribs
1   medium cucumber
2   wooden skewers (6 inches)
Fresh baby carrots and green and purple broccoli
     florets *or* vegetables of your choice
Vegetable dill dip

1 Cut celery ribs in half lengthwise and then into 6-in. pieces. Cut cucumber into 1/2-in. slices. Place one cucumber slice on the end of each skewer; place celery pieces lengthwise across skewers to form wagon frame.

2 Pile carrots, broccoli and remaining cucumber on wagon. Serve with dip.

YIELD: 4-6 SERVINGS.

gold-medal vegetable dip

Therese Judge, Westminster, Maryland

The crowd at our Olympics party declared this tangy dip a winner! With just enough zip from mustard and Worcestershire sauce, it's a great-tasting accompaniment to crisp, colorful vegetables.

 1 carton (8 ounces) spreadable chive and onion cream cheese
 2 tablespoons mayonnaise
 1 teaspoon prepared mustard
 1/2 teaspoon Worcestershire sauce
 1/4 teaspoon salt
 1/8 teaspoon pepper
 1 to 2 tablespoons milk
Assorted fresh vegetables

 1 In a small bowl, combine the cream cheese, mayonnaise, mustard, Worcestershire sauce, salt and pepper. Add enough milk until dip achieves desired consistency. Serve with vegetables.

YIELD: ABOUT 1-1/4 CUPS.

crescent butterflies

Taste of Home Test Kitchen

Kids will enjoy dipping these savory snacks in marinara sauce. A cookie cutter makes it easy to cut the butterfly shapes from crescent roll dough.

 1 tube (8 ounces) refrigerated crescent rolls
 2 giant Slim Jim snack sticks, cut into 2-inch pieces
 2 tablespoons butter, melted
 1 tablespoon grated Parmesan cheese
 1 tablespoon Italian seasoning
 1 cup marinara sauce, warmed

 1 Unroll crescent dough on a lightly floured surface; roll into a 12-in. x 9-in. rectangle. Seal seams. Cut with a butterfly cookie cutter dipped in flour. Place 1 in. apart on an ungreased baking sheet. Press a snack piece in the middle of each butterfly; carefully pinch dough around the long sides of snack piece.

 2 Brush wings with butter. Sprinkle with cheese and Italian seasoning. Bake at 375° for 10-12 minutes or until golden brown. Cool for 5 minutes before removing to a wire rack. Serve warm with marinara sauce.

YIELD: 1 DOZEN.

pepperoni roll-ups

Debra Purcell, Safford, Arizona

Here is a fast appetizer recipe that goes over well at my house. Each bite has gooey, melted cheese and real pizza flavor. Try serving with pizza sauce for dipping.

- 1 tube (8 ounces) refrigerated crescent rolls
- 16 slices pepperoni, cut into quarters
- 2 pieces string cheese (1 ounce *each*), cut into quarters
- 3/4 teaspoon Italian seasoning, *divided*
- 1/4 teaspoon garlic salt

1 Unroll crescent dough; separate into eight triangles. Place eight pepperoni pieces on each. Place a piece of cheese on the short side of each triangle; sprinkle with 1/2 teaspoon Italian seasoning. Roll up each, starting with the short side; pinch seams to seal. Sprinkle with garlic salt and remaining Italian seasoning.

2 Place 2 in. apart on a greased baking sheet. Bake at 375° for 10-12 minutes or until golden brown.

YIELD: 8 APPETIZERS.

pineapple bacon pizza

(pictured at left)

Amanda Hoffman, Worthington, Minnesota

Eating pizza is fun, but making it with your favorite ingredients is even better! One weekend when I was home from college, I made this for my family—and they thought it was amazing! Friends will love munching it on movie night.

- 1 prebaked 12-inch pizza crust
- 1/2 cup sweet-and-sour sauce
- 3/4 cup unsweetened pineapple tidbits, drained
- 1/2 cup mixed nuts, coarsely chopped
- 1 package (7 ounces) sliced Canadian bacon, chopped
- 1 cup (4 ounces) shredded reduced-fat Mexican cheese blend

1 Place the crust on an ungreased 14-in. pizza pan. Top with sauce, pineapple, nuts, bacon and cheese. Bake at 450° for 8-12 minutes or until cheese is melted. Cut into wedges.

YIELD: 6 SERVINGS.

easy buffalo chicken dip

Janice Foltz, Hershey, Pennsylvania

Guys and gals of all ages will simply devour this delicious dip. The spicy kick makes it a perfect game-day food.

- 1 package (8 ounces) reduced-fat cream cheese
- 1 cup (8 ounces) reduced-fat sour cream
- 1/2 cup Louisiana-style hot sauce
- 3 cups shredded cooked chicken breast

Assorted crackers

1 In a large bowl, beat the cream cheese, sour cream and hot sauce until smooth; stir in chicken.

2 Transfer to an 8-in. square baking dish coated with cooking spray. Cover and bake at 350° for 18-22 minutes or until heated through. Serve warm with crackers.

YIELD: 4 CUPS.

pretzels with mustard

Taste of Home Test Kitchen

The quick sauce for this wonderful treat adds an "almost homemade" note to classic chewy pretzels.

- 1/2 cup Dijon mustard
- 1/3 cup honey
- 1 tablespoon white wine vinegar
- 2 teaspoons sugar

Large soft pretzels, warmed

1 In a small bowl, whisk the mustard, honey, vinegar and sugar until blended. Serve with soft pretzels.

YIELD: 3/4 CUP.

pizza joes

(pictured at right)

Barbara Gorden, Hanover, Pennsylvania

My creation resembles a traditional sloppy Joe sandwich, but it's a lot more fun to eat!

- 1 pound Italian sausage, casings removed
- 1 medium green pepper, chopped
- 1 small onion, chopped
- 1/2 cup fresh chopped mushrooms
- 2 teaspoons Italian seasonings
- 1 clove garlic, minced
- 1 can (8 ounces) tomato sauce
- 6 English muffins, split and toasted
- 2 cups shredded mozzarella cheese

1 In a skillet, brown sausage until no longer pink; drain. Add the pepper, onion and mushrooms; cook until crisp-tender. Add Italian seasoning and garlic; cook 1 minute longer. Stir in tomato sauce and simmer, uncovered, for 10 minutes.

2 Top each muffin half with 2 tablespoons meat sauce; sprinkle with cheese. Broil until cheese melts and filling is hot. Serve immediately.

YIELD: 12 SERVINGS.

creamy ranch dip

Janice Freeman, Kewanee, Illinois

Here's a wonderfully thick and easy dip to dress up veggies, crackers or chips.

- 2 cups (16 ounces) sour cream
- 1 package (8 ounces) cream cheese, softened
- 2 envelopes ranch salad dressing mix

Fresh vegetables, crackers *or* chips

1 In a small bowl, beat the sour cream, cream cheese and ranch dressing mix on medium speed until smooth. Transfer to a serving bowl; refrigerate until serving. Serve with vegetables, crackers or chips.

YIELD: 3 CUPS.

honey peanut apple dip

Carolyn Sykora, Bloomer, Wisconsin

Everyone just loves this sweet, creamy dip—it never lasts long. It's easy to scoop up with sliced apples.

- 1 package (8 ounces) cream cheese, softened
- 1 cup finely chopped peanuts
- 2/3 cup honey
- 1 teaspoon vanilla extract

Sliced apples

1 In a bowl, beat cream cheese until smooth. Beat in the peanuts, honey and vanilla until combined. Serve with apples.

YIELD: 2 CUPS.

deluxe nachos

Jennifer Parham, Browns Summit, North Carolina

Topped with fresh veggies and sour cream, these quick and inexpensive nachos will delight family and friends.

- 2 cans (10-3/4 ounces *each*) condensed cheddar cheese soup, undiluted
- 1 cup salsa
- 2 packages (10 ounces *each*) tortilla chips
- 2 to 4 plum tomatoes, chopped
- 1 medium green pepper, chopped
- 1 medium sweet red pepper, chopped
- 4 to 6 green onions, sliced
- 2 cans (2-1/4 ounces *each*) sliced ripe olives, drained
- 1 cup (8 ounces) sour cream

1 In a small saucepan, combine soup and salsa; heat through. Arrange tortilla chips on two serving platters; top with soup mixture. Sprinkle with the tomatoes, peppers, onions and olives. Top with sour cream. Serve immediately.

YIELD: 8 SERVINGS.

fruit flower garden

(pictured at left)

Taste of Home Test Kitchen

Spruce up any summer activity with a surprisingly easy fruit platter that's as good to look at as it is to eat! In about 30 minutes, you can make this centerpiece that'll wow guests so much, they'll all be asking for your secrets!

Fresh parsley sprigs
Fresh strawberries
Sliced fresh honeydew melon, pineapple and kiwi
Seedless red grapes, halved
ANTS:
Seedless red grapes
Pretzel sticks
Dried currants
GARNISHES:
Orange slices
Orange peel strips

1 Line a large serving platter with parsley. With a small sharp knife, cut a strawberry vertically toward the cap. Repeat, cutting to form petals resembling a rose. Repeat with remaining berries.

2 Using cookie cutters, cut honeydew, pineapple and kiwi into desired shapes. Decorate with grape halves as desired.

3 For ants, skewer three grapes with a pretzel stick. With a small sharp knife, cut two small holes in a grape for eyes; insert currants. Arrange three pretzel sticks on the platter for legs; top with an ant body. Repeat as desired.

4 Decorate platter with berry roses, fruit cutouts, ants, orange slices and peel.

YIELD: 1 FRUIT FLOWER GARDEN.

cereal snack mix

Becky Larson, Duluth, Minnesota

I grew up with this mix, and now my husband and kids eat it up until it's gone. It's easy to throw together.

9 cups Crispix
1 cup Cheerios
1 cup Bugles
1 cup pretzel sticks
1 cup salted peanuts
2/3 cup butter, melted
2 tablespoons Worcestershire sauce
2 teaspoons celery salt
2 teaspoons lemon juice
1 teaspoon garlic powder

1 In a large bowl, combine the first five ingredients. In a small bowl, combine the remaining ingredients. Drizzle over cereal mixture; toss to coat.

2 Transfer to two greased 15-in. x 10-in. x 1-in. baking pans. Bake at 250° for 30 minutes, stirring every 10 minutes. Cool completely on wire racks. Store in an airtight container.

YIELD: 3-1/4 QUARTS.

gooey pizza dip

Kitti Boesel, Woodbridge, Virginia

Pepperoni, tomatoes and olives dress up my cheesy baked dip. I serve it with breadsticks and wedges of a packaged pizza crust. You can even prepare individual servings in ramekins if you like.

- 1 cup (8 ounces) reduced-fat ricotta cheese
- 1 cup fat-free mayonnaise
- 1-1/2 cups (6 ounces) shredded part-skim mozzarella cheese, *divided*
- 1/4 cup grated Parmesan cheese
- 3/4 cup diced seeded plum tomatoes, *divided*
- 1 can (2-1/2 ounces) sliced ripe olives, drained, *divided*
- 1/4 cup sliced turkey pepperoni
- 1 teaspoon garlic powder
- 1 teaspoon Italian seasoning
- 1/8 teaspoon crushed red pepper flakes
Assorted crackers

1 In a large bowl, combine the ricotta, mayonnaise, 1 cup mozzarella, Parmesan cheese, 1/2 cup tomatoes, 6 tablespoons olives, pepperoni, garlic powder, Italian seasoning and pepper flakes.

2 Spread into a 9-in. pie plate coated with cooking spray. Sprinkle with remaining mozzarella.

3 Bake at 350° for 25-30 minutes or until edges are bubbly and top is golden brown. Sprinkle with remaining tomatoes and olives. Serve with crackers.

YIELD: 3 CUPS.

healthy house

Mary Wollensak, Brookfield, Wisconsin

When my daughter Jessica was in the 3rd grade, she had an extra-credit assignment dealing with nutrition. While I was combing through cookbooks, Jessica came up with this! Everyone at school loved it, and since then, she's been eager to help in the kitchen and experiment with new recipes.

- 1 slice whole wheat bread, crust removed
- 1 tablespoon peanut butter
- 1 thin slice deli turkey
- 1 raisin
- 5 pieces Rice Chex
- 1 slice American cheese
- 1 celery stick

1 Spread bread with peanut butter. For door, cut turkey into a 1-1/2-in. x 1-1/4-in. rectangle; position on bread. Add raisin for doorknob and cereal for windows.

2 Cut the cheese slice in half diagonally; place one piece above bread for roof (save remaining piece for another use). Add celery stick for chimney.

YIELD: 1 SERVING.

15-minute caramel apple dip

Becky Heiner, West Valley City, Utah

This four-ingredient caramel dip is so simple and yummy. People always want to know how long I worked to prepare it on the stove and are amazed to find that I made it in the microwave. When large marshmallows aren't on hand, I substitute 2 cups of mini marshmallows.

1	package (14 ounces) caramels
20	large marshmallows
1/2	cup butter, melted
1/3	cup heavy whipping cream
	Apple slices

1 Place caramels in a microwave-safe bowl. Microwave, uncovered, on high for 1 minute. Add marshmallows; microwave for 1 minute or until marshmallows are melted, stirring occasionally. Whisk in butter and cream until combined. Serve with apple slices.

YIELD: 2-1/2 CUPS.

EDITOR'S NOTE: This recipe was tested in a 1,100-watt microwave.

sloppy joe nachos

Janet Rhoden, Hortonville, Wisconsin

When my kids were little, they adored these snacks they could eat with their fingers. It makes a great quick meal, tailgate food or treat when you have the munchies.

1   **pound ground beef**
1   **can (15-1/2 ounces) sloppy joe sauce**

1   **package (12 ounces) tortilla chips**
3/4   **cup shredded cheddar cheese**
1/4   **cup sliced ripe olives, optional**

1 In a large skillet, cook beef over medium heat until no longer pink; drain. Add sloppy joe sauce; cook, uncovered, for 5 minutes or until heated through.

2 Arrange tortilla chips on a serving plate. Top with meat mixture, cheese and olives if desired.

YIELD: 6 SERVINGS.

3 Cut a thin slice from the end of the top portion for the convertible top. Trim slice to fit on tail end of car; set aside. Remove fruit from both portions of melon; cut into balls or cubes and set aside. Attach convertible top with toothpicks.

4 For side mirrors, cut a 1-1/4-in. notch from each lower corner of windshield. Place a strawberry half in each notch; attach with toothpicks. For windshield, using a small sharp knife, score a 3/4-in. frame around perimeter of windshield. Carefully remove rind within frame of windshield.

5 For wheels, attach two lime slices with toothpicks to each side of melon. Cut the remaining lime slice in half. Using a toothpick, place one portion centered below windshield for a mouth.

6 For eyebrows, remove fruit from the remaining half slice; cut peel into two pieces. For eyes, cut ends from red grape. Using toothpicks, add grapes to the marshmallow halves and position on windshield; attach eyebrows. If desired, add a mandarin orange smile.

7 In a large bowl, combine the green grapes and remaining mandarin oranges with reserved watermelon. Spoon into car.

YIELD: 6-8 SERVINGS.

watermelon beetle convertible

Taste of Home Test Kitchen

What could be cooler than a convertible in the summer? You'll have as much fun as we did when we made this fun watermelon version.

1   miniature seedless watermelon (about 3 pounds)
1   fresh strawberry, halved
5   lime slices
1   seedless red grape
1   large marshmallow, cut in half
1   can (11 ounces) mandarin oranges, drained
1   cup green grapes

1 With a long sharp knife, cut a thin slice from watermelon so melon lies flat. Using a small sharp knife, lightly score a horizontal cutting line around middle of the melon, leaving 3 in. on each side of stem end unscored for the windshield. Next, score a vertical line over top of melon, connecting both ends of the horizontal line.

2 Using the long knife, cut through melon along the vertical cutting line. (Stop cutting at the horizontal cutting line.) Then, cut through melon along the horizontal cutting line. Gently pull away top portion of car.

tomato cheese pizzas

Michelle Wise, Cookeville, Tennessee

My mom used to prepare these yummy pizzas in the toaster oven for me when I was little. They're fast, healthy and delicious!

2   English muffins, split and toasted
4   slices (1 ounce *each*) process American cheese
4   slices tomato
1/2 teaspoon dried oregano

1 Place the English muffins cut side up on a broiler pan. Top with cheese and tomato; sprinkle pizzas with oregano.

2 Broil 4-6 in. from the heat for 2-3 minutes or until cheese is melted.

YIELD: 4 PIZZAS.

1 cup Cheerios
1 cup unblanched almonds
1 cup pecan halves
1/4 cup reduced-fat butter, melted
1/4 cup Worcestershire sauce
2 teaspoons chili powder
2 teaspoons paprika
1/2 teaspoon onion powder
4 to 6 drops hot pepper sauce
1/2 cup dried cranberries

1 In a large bowl, combine the cereal and nuts. Spread into two ungreased 15-in. x 10-in. x 1-in. baking pans. In a small bowl, combine the butter, Worcestershire sauce, chili powder, paprika, onion powder and pepper sauce; pour over cereal mixture and toss to coat.

2 Bake at 300° for 20 minutes, stirring once. Stir in cranberries. Cool. Store in airtight containers.

YIELD: 7 CUPS.

EDITOR'S NOTE: This recipe was tested with Land O'Lakes light stick butter.

veggie cheese people

Taste of Home Test Kitchen

These edible people let little ones get creative at the table, encouraging them to nibble as they go.

Celery rib
Grape tomatoes
Small zucchini
Yellow summer squash
Fresh sugar snap peas
Pitted ripe olives
String cheese
Seeded quartered watermelon
Wooden skewers and toothpicks

1 Cut vegetables and cheese into desired shapes. To create people, thread shapes onto skewers; use toothpicks to attach arms and legs. Insert into watermelon.

YIELD: VARIES.

nutty snack mix

Taste of Home Test Kitchen

This toasty mix is a little spicy and a whole lot tasty! It's perfect for parties or for that long car ride to Grandma's house. No matter when you serve it, this mix will be a hit!

2 cups Multi-Bran Chex
2 cups Wheat Chex

mini phyllo tacos

(pictured at right)

Roseann Weston, Philipsburg, Pennsylvania

For a winning appetizer, serve crispy phyllo cups filled with taco-seasoned ground beef and zesty shredded cheese. These little munchies are sure to be popular.

1 pound lean ground beef (90% lean)
1/2 cup finely chopped onion
1 envelope taco seasoning
3/4 cup water
1-1/4 cups shredded Mexican cheese blend, *divided*
2 packages (1.9 ounces *each*) frozen miniature phyllo tart shells

1 In a small skillet, cook beef and onion over medium heat until meat is no longer pink; drain. Stir in taco seasoning and water. Bring to a boil. Reduce heat; simmer, uncovered, for 5 minutes. Remove from the heat; stir in 1/2 cup cheese blend.

2 Place tart shells in an ungreased 15-in. x 10-in. x 1-in. baking pan. Fill with taco mixture.

3 Bake at 350° for 6 minutes. Sprinkle with remaining cheese blend; bake 2-3 minutes longer or until cheese is melted.

YIELD: 2-1/2 DOZEN.

hot pizza party fondue

(pictured at left)

Margaret Schissler, Milwaukee, Wisconsin

Great for a party or game-day gathering, this dip can be made with Italian sausage instead of ground beef.

1/2	pound ground beef
1	cup chopped fresh mushrooms
1	medium onion, chopped
1	garlic clove, minced
1	tablespoon cornstarch
1-1/2	teaspoons fennel seed
1-1/2	teaspoons dried oregano
1/4	teaspoon garlic powder
2	cans (15 ounces *each*) pizza sauce
2-1/2	cups (10 ounces) shredded cheddar cheese
1	cup (4 ounces) shredded part-skim mozzarella cheese
2	tablespoons chopped ripe olives

Breadsticks, bagel chips, baked pita chips *and/or* tortilla chips

1 In a large skillet, cook the beef, mushrooms and onion over medium heat until meat is no longer pink. Add garlic; cook 1 minute longer. Drain. Stir in the cornstarch, fennel, oregano and garlic powder until blended. Stir in pizza sauce.

2 Bring to a boil; cook and stir for 1-2 minutes or until thickened. Gradually stir in cheeses until melted. Stir in olives. Keep warm.

3 Serve with breadsticks, bagel chips, pita chips and/or tortilla chips.

YIELD: 5-1/2 CUPS.

cheese popcorn snack

Denise Baumert, Dalhart, Texas

This wonderful snack reminds me of my high school days. My sisters, girlfriends and I would stay up late, listen to music, talk and munch on this crunchy treat.

4	quarts plain popped popcorn
1/4	cup butter, melted
1/2	teaspoon garlic salt
1/2	teaspoon onion salt
2	cups (8 ounces) shredded cheddar cheese

1 Place popcorn in two 13-in. x 9-in. baking pans. Drizzle with melted butter. Combine garlic salt and onion salt; sprinkle over popcorn. Top with cheese. Bake at 300° for 5-10 minutes. Serve immediately.

YIELD: 4 QUARTS.

pbj on a stick

Sara Martin, Brookfield, Wisconsin

This is a fun way to have peanut butter and jelly! My friends love snacking on these when they come to our house.

2	peanut butter and jelly sandwiches
4	wooden skewers (5 to 6 inches)
1	cup seedless red *or* green grapes
1	small banana, sliced

1 Cut sandwiches into 1-in. squares. For each skewer, thread a grape, sandwich square and banana slice. Add another sandwich square and grape to each. Serve immediately.

YIELD: 4 SKEWERS.

ham & cheese bagel snacks

(pictured at right)

Kimberly Leman, Fairbury, Illinois

I remember having these yummy snacks as a child. They're fast and perfect as appetizers, a quick supper or even a snack!

  1   cup (4 ounces) shredded Colby cheese
1/2   cup diced deli ham
1/2   cup mayonnaise
  4   bacon strips, cooked and crumbled
  6   miniature bagels, split

1 In a small bowl, combine the first four ingredients. Spread over bagels. Place on an ungreased baking sheet.

2 Broil 4-6 in. from the heat for 2-4 minutes or until lightly browned and bubbly.

YIELD: 1 DOZEN.

odds 'n' ends snack mix

Terry Kuehn, Waunakee, Wisconsin

Cayenne pepper packs some punch in this irresistible blend of cereal, pretzels, peanuts and cute fish-shaped crackers! This makes a big batch, so it's perfect to keep on hand for anytime snacking.

  4   cups Corn Chex
  4   cups Rice Chex
  4   cups Wheat Chex
  1   package (10 ounces) pretzel sticks
  2   cups dry roasted peanuts
  1   package (6 ounces) miniature fish-shaped crackers
  1   cup butter, melted
1/4   cup Worcestershire sauce
  1   teaspoon seasoned salt
1/8   to 1/4 teaspoon cayenne pepper

1 In a large bowl, combine the first six ingredients. In a small bowl, combine the butter, Worcestershire sauce, seasoned salt and cayenne; pour over cereal mixture and stir to coat. Spread into two greased 15-in. x 10-in. x 1-in. baking pans. Bake at 300° for 1 hour, stirring every 15 minutes. Spread on paper towels to cool. Store in airtight containers.

YIELD: ABOUT 4 QUARTS.

little hawaiian pizzas

Vicky Priestley, Alum Creek, West Virginia

These little English muffin pizzas are a perfect after-school snack that kids of all ages will enjoy.

  2   English muffins, split and toasted
  2   tablespoons barbecue sauce
  2   ounces sliced deli ham, cut into strips
  1   snack-size cup (4 ounces) pineapple tidbits, well drained
  2   slices (1 ounce *each*) Swiss cheese, quartered

1 Place English muffins cut side up on a broiler pan. Spread with barbecue sauce; top with ham, pineapple and cheese. Broil 4-6 in. from the heat for 2-3 minutes or until cheese is melted.

YIELD: 4 PIZZAS.

apple cartwheels

(pictured at left)

Miriam Miller, Thorp, Wisconsin

When you need to feed a group of children, try these stuffed apple rings. The yummy filling is an irresistible combination of creamy peanut butter, sweet honey, miniature chocolate chips and raisins.

- 1/4 cup peanut butter
- 1-1/2 teaspoons honey
- 1/2 cup miniature semisweet chocolate chips
- 2 tablespoons raisins
- 4 medium Red Delicious apples, cored

1 In a small bowl, combine peanut butter and honey; fold in chocolate chips and raisins.

2 Fill centers of apples with peanut butter mixture; refrigerate for at least 1 hour. Cut into 1/4-in. rings.

YIELD: ABOUT 2 DOZEN.

fun-on-the-run snack mix

Carrie Hubbard, Buena Vista, Colorado

My kids love this and have no idea they're eating cranberries. It's a great healthy snack for car rides, hikes or picnics.

- 2 cups Wheat Chex
- 2 cups miniature fish-shaped crackers
- 2 cups pretzel sticks
- 1 cup salted peanuts
- 1 cup dried cranberries

1 In a large bowl, combine the cereal, crackers, pretzels, peanuts and cranberries. Store in an airtight container.

YIELD: 8 CUPS.

chicken chili nachos

Karen Horning, Rockford, Illinois

These spicy nachos have plenty of chicken and two kinds of beans, so they make an amazing party snack.

- 1 pound boneless skinless chicken breasts, cubed
- 1 can (10 ounces) diced tomatoes and green chilies, undrained
- 1 can (16 ounces) kidney beans, rinsed and drained
- 1 can (16 ounces) chili beans, undrained
- 1 teaspoon paprika
- 1 teaspoon ground cumin
- 1/2 teaspoon cayenne pepper
- 1 package (13-1/2 ounces) tortilla chips
- 1-1/2 cups (6 ounces) shredded Mexican cheese blend

1 In a large skillet coated with cooking spray, cook chicken until no longer pink. Add tomatoes; cook over medium-high heat for 3 minutes or until tomato juice is reduced. Stir in the beans, paprika, cumin and cayenne; heat through.

2 Arrange the tortilla chips on two large microwave-safe plates; sprinkle each with 1/4 cup cheese. Top with chicken mixture and remaining cheese. Microwave, uncovered, on high for 25-30 seconds or until cheese is melted.

YIELD: 8 SERVINGS.

italian dipping sticks

(pictured at right)

Michelle Revelle, Guyton, Georgia

These dressed-up breadsticks are a favorite snack in our house during the Super Bowl. It's fun to dip them in warm pizza sauce.

1	tube (11 ounces) refrigerated breadsticks
1/4	cup grated Parmesan cheese
1/2	teaspoon Italian seasoning
1	cup pizza sauce
1/4	cup shredded part-skim mozzarella cheese

1 Unroll breadstick dough; cut each piece in half widthwise and separate. In a large resealable plastic bag, combine Parmesan cheese and Italian seasoning. Add dough pieces, a few at a time, and shake to coat.

2 Place on an ungreased baking sheet. Bake at 375° for 10-13 minutes or until golden brown.

3 Meanwhile, place pizza sauce in a microwave-safe bowl. Cover; microwave on high for 1-2 minutes or until bubbly. Sprinkle with mozzarella cheese. Microwave 1 minute longer or until cheese is melted. Serve with breadsticks.

YIELD: 2 DOZEN.

scooter snacks

Didi Desjardins, Dartmouth, Massachusetts

Feel like building a little fun into after-school routines? Let the kids help you construct these nutritious scooter snacks to rev up their homework efforts or tide them over till suppertime!

6	pretzel sticks, *divided*
8	slices zucchini (1/4 inch thick)
2	pieces string cheese (1 ounce *each*)
2	pretzel rods, cut into 3-inch pieces
2	tablespoons spreadable garden vegetable cream cheese
4	cherry tomatoes, halved
2	pimiento-stuffed olives, halved

1 For each of four axles, thread a pretzel stick through two zucchini slices, leaving a 1-in. space in the center. For each scooter, position string cheese between two axles.

2 Attach a pretzel rod with cream cheese to each scooter; top each with a pretzel stick for handlebars. Add tomato hubcaps and olive headlights and taillights with cream cheese.

YIELD: 2 SCOOTERS.

snack crackers

Sue Manel, Milladore, Wisconsin

When the children were at home, our daughter, Dana, loved making this crunchy and flavorful snack for us. Her four older brothers would finish off a batch in no time.

3/4	cup canola oil
1-1/2	teaspoons dill weed
1	envelope (1 ounce) ranch salad dressing mix
2	packages (10 ounces *each*) oyster crackers

1 In a small bowl, whisk the oil, dill and salad dressing mix. Place the crackers in a large bowl; pour dressing mixture over crackers and toss gently to coat. Allow to stand at least 1 hour before serving.

YIELD: 12 CUPS.

sweet treats

Dash salt
1/2   teaspoon cinnamon oil
  3   to 4 drops red food coloring
 12   lollipop sticks

1 Butter 12 assorted 3-in. metal cookie cutters. Place on a parchment paper-lined baking sheet; set aside.

2 In a large heavy saucepan, combine the sugar, corn syrup and salt. Cook and stir over medium heat until sugar is dissolved. Bring to a boil; cook, without stirring, until a candy thermometer reads 300° (hard-crack stage).

3 Remove from the heat; stir in oil and food coloring (keep face away from mixture as oil is very strong). Immediately pour sugar mixture into prepared cutters.

4 Remove cutters just before lollipops are set; firmly press a lollipop stick into each. Cool completely. Store in an airtight container.

YIELD: 1 DOZEN.

EDITOR'S NOTE: We recommend that you test your candy thermometer before each use by bringing water to a boil; the thermometer should read 212°. Adjust your recipe temperature up or down based on your test.

caramel apple slushies

Taste of Home Test Kitchen

This spirited slushie captures the sweet fall flavor of caramel apples!

  1   medium apple, peeled and sliced
1/2   cup thawed apple juice concentrate
  5   teaspoons caramel ice cream topping
1/4   teaspoon lemon juice
  7   ice cubes
Additional caramel ice cream topping, optional

1 In a blender, combine the apple, juice concentrate, ice cream topping and lemon juice; cover and process until blended. Add ice cubes; cover and process until smooth. Pour into chilled glasses. Drizzle with additional caramel topping if desired; serve immediately.

YIELD: 2 SERVINGS.

cinnamon lollipops

Sheryl Salisbury, Weatherford, Oklahoma

Fans of cinnamon will fall head over heels for these festive lollipops. Make them throughout the year using different cookie cutter shapes.

  1   cup sugar
1/2   cup light corn syrup

homemade fudge pops

Lyssa Prasek, Vita, Manitoba

On hot summer days, these are my kids' favorite frozen treats. I like that I know exactly what's in these pops, and that they're economical, too.

1/4   cup butter, cubed
1/2   cup all-purpose flour
  4   cups milk
1-1/3 cups packed brown sugar
1/3   cup baking cocoa
  1   teaspoon salt
  2   teaspoons vanilla extract
 20   Popsicle molds *or* disposable plastic cups
       (3 ounces *each*) and Popsicle sticks

1 In a large saucepan, melt butter over medium heat. Stir in flour until smooth; gradually add milk. Stir in the brown sugar, cocoa and salt. Bring to a boil; cook and stir for 2 minutes or until thickened.

2 Remove from the heat; stir in vanilla. Cool for 20 minutes, stirring several times.

3 Pour 1/4 cupfuls into Popsicle molds or plastic cups; top molds with holders or insert Popsicle sticks into cups. Freeze until firm.

YIELD: 20 SERVINGS.

chocolate malt crispy bars

Taste of Home Test Kitchen

This chunky, chewy square is a feast for the eyes. Malted milk flavor coats this bar from top to bottom.

  4   cups malted milk balls, *divided*
  1   package (10 ounces) large marshmallows
  3   tablespoons butter
  5   cups crisp rice cereal
  1   cup malted milk powder, *divided*
  2   cups (12 ounces) semisweet chocolate chips

1 Chop 1 cup malted milk balls; set aside. In a Dutch oven, combine marshmallows and butter. Cook and stir over medium-low heat until melted. Remove from the heat; stir in the cereal, 3/4 cup malt powder and chopped candy. Press into a greased 13-in. x 9-in. pan.

2 In a microwave-safe bowl, melt chocolate chips; stir until smooth. Stir in the remaining malt powder. Spread over cereal bars. Top with remaining malted milk balls. Let stand until set. Cut into squares.

YIELD: 2 DOZEN.

hidden treasure cupcakes

Taste of Home Test Kitchen

Let kids discover the hidden treasure inside these cute-as-can-be cupcakes! They're make-ahead convenient and ensure even portions for all party guests! They'd be great for any ocean-themed celebration.

- 1 package (18-1/4 ounces) chocolate cake mix
- 1/4 cup strawberry pie filling
- 24 Swiss cake rolls
- 1 can (16 ounces) vanilla frosting
- Blue food coloring, optional
- Assorted candies: Jolly Ranchers, Nerds, skull and fish hard candies
- Yellow food coloring, optional

1 Prepare cake mix according to package directions. Fill paper-lined muffin cups half full. Drop 1/2 teaspoon pie filling in the center of each; top with remaining batter.

2 Bake at 350° for 18-22 minutes or until a toothpick inserted in the cake portion comes out clean. Cool for 10 minutes before removing from pans to wire racks to cool completely.

3 Meanwhile, cut cake rolls lengthwise (do not cut through); set aside. Place two tablespoons frosting in a small bowl; set aside. Tint remaining frosting with blue food coloring if desired; frost cupcakes.

4 Place a cake roll on each cupcake. Decorate with assorted candies. Tint reserved frosting with yellow food coloring if desired; place in a resealable plastic bag. Cut a small hole in a corner of bag; pipe latches onto chests.

YIELD: 24 SERVINGS.

gingerbread cookies

(pictured at left)

Christy Thelen, Kellogg, Iowa

My kids linger around the kitchen when these delightfully aromatic cookies are baking. I make them throughout the year using a variety of holiday-themed cookie cutters. Decorating them can be so much fun. Let the whole gang get in on the act!

3/4 cup butter, softened
1 cup packed brown sugar
1 egg
3/4 cup molasses
4 cups all-purpose flour
2 teaspoons ground ginger
1-1/2 teaspoons baking soda
1-1/2 teaspoons ground cinnamon
3/4 teaspoon ground cloves
1/4 teaspoon salt
Vanilla frosting of your choice
Paste food coloring of your choice

1 In a large bowl, cream butter and brown sugar until light and fluffy. Beat in egg and molasses. Combine the flour, ginger, baking soda, cinnamon, cloves and salt; gradually add to creamed mixture and mix well. Cover and refrigerate for 4 hours or until easy to handle.

2 On a lightly floured surface, roll dough to 1/8-in. thickness. Cut with a floured 3-1/2-in. gingerbread man cookie cutter. Place 2 in. apart on ungreased baking sheets.

3 Reroll scraps; cut out sixty 1-1/4-in. triangles. Place triangles on heads for hats. Using remaining scraps, roll sixty 1/4-in. balls; place on top of hats for pom-poms. Gently press to seal edges.

4 Bake the cookies at 350° for 8-10 minutes or until edges are firm. Remove to wire racks to cool.

5 Tint some of the frosting as desired; use to decorate cookies with hats and buttons. Decorate the cookies with cuffs, faces and fluffy pom-poms with the white frosting.

YIELD: 5 DOZEN.

blueberry fruit smoothies

Mary Walton, Woodland, Washington

This low-fat but yummy smoothie feels like an old-fashioned treat from a soda fountain. You'll fall for its gorgeous color.

1 cup reduced-fat vanilla ice cream
1 cup fresh *or* frozen blueberries
1/2 cup chopped peeled fresh peaches *or* frozen unsweetened sliced peaches
1/2 cup pineapple juice
1/4 cup vanilla yogurt

1 In a blender, combine all ingredients; cover and process until smooth. Pour into chilled glasses; serve immediately.

YIELD: 3 SERVINGS.

pink velvet cupcakes

(pictured at right)

Paulette Smith, Winston-Salem, North Carolina

Pretty in pink, these cupcakes were a big success at my daughter's princess-themed birthday party. They would be perfect for gatherings throughout the year, too!

```
  1   cup butter, softened
1-1/4 cups sugar
  1/8 teaspoon pink paste food coloring
  3   eggs
  1   teaspoon vanilla extract
2-1/2 cups all-purpose flour
1-1/2 teaspoons baking powder
  1/4 teaspoon baking soda
  1/4 teaspoon salt
  1   cup buttermilk
```
WHITE CHOCOLATE GANACHE:
```
  2   cups white baking chips
  1/2 cup heavy whipping cream
  1   tablespoon butter
```
Pink coarse sugar and edible glitter

1 In a large bowl, cream the butter, sugar and food coloring until light and fluffy. Add eggs, one at a time, beating well after each addition. Beat in vanilla. Combine the flour, baking powder, baking soda and salt; add to creamed mixture alternately with buttermilk, beating well after each addition.

2 Fill paper-lined muffin cups two-thirds full. Bake at 350° for 23-27 minutes or until a toothpick inserted near the center comes out clean. Cool for 10 minutes before removing from pans to wire racks to cool completely.

3 Meanwhile, place white chips in a small bowl. In a small saucepan, bring cream just to a boil. Pour over chips; whisk until smooth. Stir in butter. Transfer to a large bowl. Chill for 30 minutes, stirring once.

4 Beat on high speed for 2-3 minutes or until soft peaks form and frosting is light and fluffy. Cut a small hole in the corner of a pastry or plastic bag; insert #30 star tip. Fill bag with frosting; frost cupcakes. Sprinkle with coarse sugar and edible glitter. Store in the refrigerator.

YIELD: 2 DOZEN.

EDITOR'S NOTE: Edible glitter is available from Wilton Industries. Call 800-794-5866 or visit wilton.com.

cinnamon roll bunnies

Taste of Home Test Kitchen

A tube of purchased cinnamon roll dough and a little imagination make these adorable bunnies almost too cute to eat! These little treats will definitely appeal to "somebunny" at your house!

```
  1   tube (12.4 ounces) refrigerated cinnamon
      roll dough
 12   M&M's miniature baking bits
  4   pink jelly beans
 24   pieces black shoestring licorice (1 inch)
  1   drop red food coloring
```
Brown decorating gel *or* color of your choice

1 Separate dough into eight rolls. Place four rolls on a greased baking sheet. Using a 2-in. biscuit cutter, cut 3/4 in. into both sides of remaining rolls to form ears and bow ties. Place ears at the top and a bow tie below each cinnamon roll; pinch to attach. Slightly flatten rolls.

2 Bake at 400° for 8-10 minutes or until golden brown. Set aside 1-1/2 teaspoons icing. Spread remaining icing over bunnies. Place a baking bit in the center of each bow tie; add remaining baking bits for eyes. Place a jelly bean in each center for nose; attach licorice pieces for whiskers.

3 Tint reserved icing pink with red food coloring; pipe mouths and outline ears. Pipe edges of bow ties with decorating gel.

YIELD: 4 SERVINGS.

pumpkin patch torte

(pictured at left)

Taste of Home Test Kitchen

This cake is unforgettably moist, delicious and not too sweet. The frosting's subtle maple flavor is the perfect accompaniment to the pumpkin cake.

- 1 can (15 ounces) solid-pack pumpkin
- 1 cup packed brown sugar
- 1/2 cup sugar
- 4 eggs
- 1/2 cup canola oil
- 2 cups all-purpose flour
- 1 teaspoon baking powder
- 1 teaspoon baking soda
- 1 teaspoon ground cinnamon
- 1 teaspoon ground ginger
- 1/2 teaspoon salt

FROSTING:
- 1 cup maple syrup
- 2 egg whites
- 1/4 teaspoon cream of tartar
- 3 drops green food coloring
- 1 drop yellow food coloring
- Candy pumpkins

1 Line a greased 15-in. x 10-in. x 1-in. baking pan with waxed paper; grease the paper. In a large bowl, beat the pumpkin, sugars, eggs and oil until well blended. Combine the flour, baking powder, baking soda, cinnamon, ginger and salt; gradually add to pumpkin mixture. Pour batter into prepared pan.

2 Bake at 350° for 20-25 minutes or until a toothpick inserted near the center comes out clean. Cool for 5 minutes before inverting onto a wire rack to cool completely. Carefully remove waxed paper.

3 For frosting, in a large heavy saucepan over low heat, combine the syrup, egg whites and cream of tartar. With a portable mixer, beat on low speed for 1 minute. Continue beating until frosting reaches 160°, about 8 minutes. Transfer to a large bowl. Beat on high speed until frosting forms stiff peaks, about 7 minutes. Remove 1/4 cup frosting to a small bowl; tint with green and yellow food coloring and set aside.

4 Cut cake widthwise into thirds. Place one layer on a serving plate; spread with a third of the frosting. Repeat layers. Arrange pumpkins on cake; add vines with the green frosting.

YIELD: 12 SERVINGS.

monkey muffins

Amie Longstaff, Painesville Township, Ohio

These bite-sized mini muffins will be a favorite. The recipe makes a lot, so you'll have plenty to share with friends.

- 1/2 cup butter, softened
- 1 cup plus 1 tablespoon sugar, *divided*
- 2 eggs
- 1 cup mashed ripe bananas
- 2/3 cup peanut butter
- 1 tablespoon milk
- 1 teaspoon vanilla extract
- 2 cups all-purpose flour
- 1 teaspoon baking soda
- 1/2 teaspoon salt
- 3/4 cup miniature semisweet chocolate chips

1 In a large bowl, cream butter and 1 cup sugar until light and fluffy. Add eggs, one at a time, beating well after each addition. Beat in the bananas, peanut butter, milk and vanilla. Combine the flour, baking soda and salt; add to creamed mixture just until moistened. Fold in chips.

2 Fill greased or paper-lined miniature muffin cups three-fourths full. Sprinkle with remaining sugar. Bake at 350° for 14-16 minutes or until a toothpick inserted near the center comes out clean. Cool for 5 minutes before removing from pans to wire racks. Serve warm.

YIELD: 6 DOZEN.

1. In a small bowl, cream butter and sugar until light and fluffy. Beat in egg. Combine the flour, baking powder, salt and baking soda; add to creamed mixture alternately with yogurt, beating well after each addition. Fold in blueberries and orange peel.

2. Fill paper-lined muffin cups three-fourths full. Bake at 375° for 20-25 minutes or until a toothpick inserted near the center comes out clean. Cool for 5 minutes before removing from pan to a wire rack. Serve warm. Leftovers may be frozen.

YIELD: 8 MUFFINS.

EDITOR'S NOTE: If using frozen blueberries, use without thawing to avoid discoloring the batter.

blueberry peach muffins

(pictured at right)

Patricia Ford, Joussard, Alberta

These mouthwatering blueberry muffins get a flavor boost from peach yogurt and orange peel. The recipe makes a nice little batch. Enjoy!

1/4	cup butter, softened
1/3	cup sugar
1	egg
1-1/4	cups all-purpose flour
1	teaspoon baking powder
1/4	teaspoon salt
1/8	teaspoon baking soda
1/2	cup peach yogurt
2/3	cup fresh *or* frozen blueberries
1	teaspoon grated orange peel

hedgehog cookies

Pam Goodlet, Washington Island, Wisconsin

Unlike the real woodland creatures, these chocolate-coated hedgehogs dwell on snack plates and cookie trays. The little guys are fun to make and eat.

1/3   cup butter, softened
1/4   cup confectioners' sugar
1/2   teaspoon vanilla extract
2/3   cup all-purpose flour
2/3   cup ground pecans
1/8   teaspoon salt
1/2   cup 60% cacao bittersweet chocolate baking chips
1/4   cup chocolate sprinkles

1   In a small bowl, cream butter and confectioners' sugar until light and fluffy. Beat in vanilla. Combine the flour, pecans and salt; gradually add to creamed mixture and mix well. Shape 1 tablespoon of dough into a ball; pinch the dough to form a face. Repeat. Place 2 in. apart on a greased baking sheet.

2   Bake at 325° for 12-15 minutes or until lightly browned. Let stand for 5 minutes before removing to a wire rack to cool completely.

3   In a microwave, melt chocolate; stir until smooth. Holding a hedgehog cookie by the nose, spoon chocolate over the back (leave the face uncovered). Allow excess to drip off. Place on waxed paper; immediately coat the wet chocolate with sprinkles.

4   With a toothpick dipped in chocolate, make two eyes and a dot on the nose. Let stand until set. Store in an airtight container.

YIELD: 16 COOKIES.

strawberry banana shakes

Grant Dixon, Roseburg, Oregon

These not-too-sweet shakes pack a strawberry-banana punch. I especially like them topped with whipped cream and fresh strawberries.

1/4	cup milk
1	cup strawberry ice cream
1	medium firm banana, sliced

Whipped cream and two fresh strawberries, optional

1 Place milk, ice cream and banana in a blender; cover and process until smooth. Pour into glasses. Garnish each shake with whipped cream and a strawberry if desired.

YIELD: 2 SERVINGS.

oatmeal chip cookies

Ruth Ann Stelfox, Raymond, Alberta

These delicious cookies use lots of oatmeal. They're crisp on the outside, sweet and chewy inside.

2	cups butter, softened
2	cups sugar
2	cups packed brown sugar
4	eggs
2	teaspoons vanilla extract
6	cups quick-cooking oats
3	cups all-purpose flour
2	teaspoons baking soda
1	teaspoon salt
2	cups (12 ounces) semisweet chocolate chips

1 In a large bowl, cream butter and sugars until light and fluffy. Beat in eggs and vanilla. Combine the oats, flour, baking soda and salt; gradually add to creamed mixture and mix well. Stir in chocolate chips. Chill dough for 1 hour or until firm.

2 Roll dough into 1-1/2 in. balls; place on greased baking sheets. Bake at 350° for 11-13 minutes or until lightly browned. Cool on wire racks.

YIELD: ABOUT 7 DOZEN.

s'more bars

Lisa Moriarty, Wilton, New Hampshire

Once school starts, it can be hard for kids to let go of summer. But these rich, gooey, great-tasting bars will bring back sweet campfire memories.

1/2	cup butter, softened
3/4	cup sugar
1	egg
1	teaspoon vanilla extract
1-1/3	cups all-purpose flour
3/4	cup graham cracker crumbs
1	teaspoon baking powder
1/8	teaspoon salt
5	milk chocolate candy bars (1.55 ounces *each*)
1	cup marshmallow creme

1 In a large bowl, cream butter and sugar until light and fluffy. Beat in egg and vanilla. Combine the flour, cracker crumbs, baking powder and salt; gradually add to creamed mixture. Set aside 1/2 cup for topping.

2 Press remaining mixture into a greased 9-in. square baking pan. Place candy bars over crust; spread with marshmallow creme. Crumble remaining graham cracker mixture over top.

3 Bake at 350° for 25-30 minutes or until golden brown. Cool on a wire rack. Cut into bars. Store in an airtight container.

YIELD: 1-1/2 DOZEN.

dragonfly snacks

Taste of Home Test Kitchen

You won't need a net to catch these delightful dragonflies, but they're so cute they'll disappear fast. Store-bought cookies and pretzels are dipped in candy coating and sprinkled with sugar.

8	ounces white candy coating, finely chopped
6	Pirouette cookies
	Colored sugar
12	pretzels
12	large marshmallows

1 Line an ungreased baking sheet with waxed paper; set aside. In a microwave, melt candy coating; stir until smooth.

2 Coat cookies with candy coating. Place on prepared pan. Sprinkle with colored sugar. Freeze for 15 minutes or until firm.

3 If necessary, warm remaining candy coating. Dip the pretzels in the coating; allow excess to drip off. Press two pretzels against each cookie, propping with the marshmallows. Immediately sprinkle with colored sugar. Let stand until set. Gently remove dragonflies from waxed paper and marshmallows.

YIELD: 6 SERVINGS.

2. Remove from the heat; stir in gelatin and sugar until dissolved. Stir in sliced strawberries. Pour into the crust. Cover and refrigerate for 2 hours or until firm.

3. Cut reserved strawberries in half. Garnish each serving with whipped topping and a berry half.

YIELD: 8 SERVINGS.

peppermint taffy

Suzette Jury, Keene, California

This candy brings back many warm memories of my grandmother. I used to help her pull this taffy every Christmas Eve. Pulled taffy makes for a wonderful cooking lesson.

- 1 tablespoon plus 1/4 cup butter, cubed
- 2 cups light corn syrup
- 1-1/2 cups sugar
- 2 teaspoons peppermint extract
- 1/2 teaspoon salt
- 6 drops red food coloring

1. Grease a 15-in. x 10-in. x 1-in. pan with 1 tablespoon butter; set aside.

2. In a small heavy saucepan, combine the corn syrup and sugar. Bring to a boil over medium heat. Add remaining butter; stir until melted. Cook and stir mixture until a candy thermometer reads 250° (hard-ball stage).

3. Remove from the heat; stir in the extract, salt and food coloring. Pour into prepared pan. Let stand for 5-10 minutes or until cool enough to handle. Divide into four portions.

4. With well-buttered fingers, quickly pull one portion of candy until firm but pliable (color will become light pink). Pull into a 1/2-in.-wide rope. Repeat with remaining candy.

5. Cut into 1-in. pieces. Wrap each in waxed paper.

YIELD: 1-3/4 POUNDS.

EDITOR'S NOTE: We recommend that you test your candy thermometer before each use by bringing water to a boil; the thermometer should read 212°. Adjust your recipe temperature up or down based on your test.

strawberry pie

D. Smith, Featerville-Trevose, Pennsylvania

There's plenty of sweet berry flavor in this refreshing dessert that just says "summer." I sometimes substitute fresh peaches and peach gelatin for an equally pretty summertime treat.

- 2 pints fresh strawberries, hulled
- 2 tablespoons cornstarch
- 1-1/2 cups cold water
- 1 package (.3 ounce) sugar-free strawberry gelatin
- 3 tablespoons sugar
- 1 reduced-fat graham cracker crust (8 inches)
- 2 cups reduced-fat whipped topping

1. Set aside four whole berries for garnish. Slice remaining strawberries and set aside. In a large saucepan, combine cornstarch and water until smooth. Bring to a boil; cook and stir for 2 minutes or until thickened.

farm friend cupcakes

(pictured at left)

Colleen Palmer, Epping, New Hampshire

These chick and pig cupcakes just can't get more adorable. Young children are especially taken with them!

- 1 package (18-1/4 ounces) devil's food cake mix
- 3 cans (16 ounces *each*) vanilla frosting
- Pink and yellow paste food coloring
- M&M's miniature baking bits
- Assorted candies (Brach's white dessert mints, pink mint candy lozenges, Good & Plenty candies and candy corn)

1 Prepare cake batter according to package directions. Fill 24 paper-lined muffin cups two-thirds full.

2 Bake at 350° for 21-26 minutes or until a toothpick inserted near the center comes out clean. Cool for 10 minutes before removing from pans to wire racks. Cool completely.

3 For pigs, tint 1 can of frosting pink; frost 12 cupcakes. Attach baking bits and dessert mints for eyes, pink candy lozenges for snouts, baking bits for nostrils and Good & Plenty candies for ears.

4 For chicks, tint 2-1/2 cups frosting yellow; transfer to a pastry bag. Insert #17 star tip; pipe frosting onto 12 cupcakes. Pipe heads and wings. Attach baking bits and dessert mints for eyes and candy corn for beaks.

YIELD: 2 DOZEN.

moo-cow cupcakes

(pictured at left)

Colleen Palmer, Epping, New Hampshire

No one will be able to resist these adorable cupcakes with pink accents on their little noses and ears! They will be a hit at any party.

- 1 package (18-1/4 ounces) devil's food cake mix
- 1 can (16 ounces) vanilla frosting
- Pink paste food coloring
- 1 can (16 ounces) chocolate frosting
- Assorted decorations: Semisweet chocolate chips, miniature semisweet chocolate chips and halved miniature marshmallows

1 Prepare cake batter according to package directions. Fill 24 paper-lined muffin cups two-thirds full.

2 Bake at 350° for 21-26 minutes or until a toothpick inserted near the center comes out clean. Cool for 10 minutes before removing from pans to wire racks to cool completely.

3 Tint 1/4 cup vanilla frosting pink; set aside. With the remaining white frosting, create a white face-shaped stripe down the center of each cupcake. Fill in the unfrosted portions with the chocolate frosting to cover cupcakes.

4 Attach chocolate chips for eyes, miniature chips for noses and marshmallow halves for ears. With reserved pink frosting, create mouths and fill in ears.

YIELD: 2 DOZEN.

speedy brownies

Diane Heier, Harwood, North Dakota

Since you dump all the ingredients together for these delicious chocolatey brownies, they take very little time to prepare. There's no mistaking the homemade goodness of a freshly baked batch. They are so rich and fudgy! And because they use pantry ingredients, you can enjoy them any time.

- 2 cups sugar
- 1-3/4 cups all-purpose flour
- 1/2 cup baking cocoa
- 1 teaspoon salt
- 5 eggs
- 1 cup canola oil
- 1 teaspoon vanilla extract
- 1 cup (6 ounces) semisweet chocolate chips

1 In a large bowl, beat the first seven ingredients. Pour into a greased 13-in. x 9-in. baking pan. Sprinkle with chocolate chips.

2 Bake at 350° for 30 minutes or until a toothpick inserted near the center comes out clean.

3 Cool in pan on a wire rack.

YIELD: ABOUT 3 DOZEN.

3 In a microwave, melt vanilla chips and shortening; stir until smooth. Drizzle over the top. Refrigerate until firm, about 1-1/2 hours. Remove from waxed paper. Let stand for 10 minutes at room temperature before cutting.

YIELD: 1-3/4 POUNDS.

chocolate cherry smoothies

Deborah Allsbrooks, Charlotte, Tennessee

Combine sweet cherries with the rich flavor of chocolate milk for a quick treat you can enjoy anytime.

- 1 cup 2% chocolate milk
- 1 cup frozen pitted dark sweet cherries
- 1 carton (4 ounces) whipped chocolate mousse yogurt
- 4 ice cubes

1 In a blender, combine all ingredients; cover and process until smooth. Pour into chilled glasses; serve immediately.

YIELD: 2 SERVINGS.

chocolate pizza heart

Becky Thesman, Enid, Oklahoma

I found this recipe in an old cookbook and changed a few ingredients to suit my family's taste. They really enjoy this candy. You'll love how fast, fun and simple it is! Get the kids to help you spread the toppings.

1-1/2 cups milk chocolate chips
- 1 cup butterscotch chips
- 3/4 cup miniature marshmallows
- 3/4 cup chopped salted peanuts
- 3/4 cup crushed potato chips
- 2 tablespoons flaked coconut
- 7 maraschino cherries, halved
- 1/4 cup milk chocolate M&M's
- 2 tablespoons vanilla *or* white chips
- 1/2 teaspoon shortening

1 Using a pencil, draw a 10-in. heart on waxed paper. Place paper, pencil mark down, on a baking sheet; set aside.

2 In a large microwave-safe bowl, melt chocolate chips and butterscotch chips; stir until smooth. Stir in the marshmallows, peanuts and potato chips. Immediately spread on prepared pan into heart shape. Sprinkle with coconut; top with cherries and M&M's.

lemon fruit dip

Megan Wilkinson, Morgan, Utah

My husband's a construction worker, and this is a great treat to put in his lunch with whatever fresh fruit he wants. It keeps all week in the fridge.

- 1 cup cold milk
- 1 package (3.4 ounces) instant lemon pudding mix
- 1 cup (8 ounces) sour cream
Assorted fresh fruit

1 In a small bowl, whisk milk and pudding mix for 2 minutes. Let stand for 2 minutes or until soft-set. Whisk in sour cream. Chill until serving. Serve with fruit.

YIELD: ABOUT 2 CUPS.

peanut butter clusters

(pictured at left)

Pat Maxwell, Taft, California

Four ingredients and 20 minutes make for one fabulous treat! This chocolate-coated crunch also freezes well, so try keeping some on hand.

- 2 cups peanut butter chips
- 1 cup milk chocolate chips
- 1-1/2 cups dry roasted peanuts
- 1 cup crushed ridged potato chips

1 In a microwave-safe bowl, melt peanut butter chips and chocolate chips; stir until smooth. Stir in the peanuts and potato chips. Drop by level tablespoonfuls onto waxed paper-lined baking sheets. Refrigerate until firm. Store in an airtight container.

YIELD: ABOUT 3-1/2 DOZEN.

EDITOR'S NOTE: This recipe was tested in a 1,100-watt microwave.

marshmallow fruit dip

Cindy Steffen, Cedarburg, Wisconsin

You can whip up this sweet and creamy dip in just ten minutes! I like to serve it in a bowl surrounded by fresh strawberries at spring brunches or luncheons.

- 1 package (8 ounces) cream cheese, softened
- 3/4 cup (6 ounces) cherry yogurt
- 1 carton (8 ounces) frozen whipped topping, thawed
- 1 jar (7 ounces) marshmallow creme
- Assorted fresh fruit

1 In a large bowl, beat cream cheese and yogurt until blended. Fold in whipped topping and marshmallow creme. Serve with fruit.

YIELD: 5 CUPS.

chocolate chocolate chip muffins

Theresa Harrington, Sheridan, Wyoming

The title says it all! These extra chocolaty muffins feature nutritious ingredients like whole wheat flour and applesauce to make a lighter muffin without sacrificing any flavor. Because they are surprisingly healthy, we even serve these for breakfast at the school where I work.

- 2-1/2 cups all-purpose flour
- 1-3/4 cups whole wheat flour
- 1-3/4 cups packed brown sugar
- 1/2 cup baking cocoa
- 1-1/4 teaspoons salt
- 1 teaspoon baking powder
- 1 teaspoon baking soda
- 2 egg whites
- 1 egg
- 2 cups unsweetened applesauce
- 1-3/4 cups fat-free milk
- 2 tablespoons canola oil
- 2-1/2 teaspoons vanilla extract
- 1-1/4 cups semisweet chocolate chips

1 In a bowl, combine the flours, brown sugar, cocoa, salt, baking powder and baking soda. In another bowl, whisk the egg whites, egg, applesauce, milk, oil and vanilla. Stir into dry ingredients just until moistened. Fold in chocolate chips.

2 Coat muffin cups with cooking spray; fill three-fourths full with batter. Bake at 350° for 18-20 minutes or until a toothpick inserted near the center comes out clean. Cool for 5 minutes before removing from pans to wire racks. Serve warm.

YIELD: 32 MUFFINS.

frozen banana split pie

Joy Collins, Birmingham, Alabama

This dessert is special enough to make hamburgers and fries a meal to remember! It's so tall and pretty and just like eating a frozen banana split. Make it ahead to save time.

- 3 tablespoons chocolate hard-shell ice cream topping
- 1 graham cracker crust (9 inches)
- 2 medium bananas, sliced
- 1/2 teaspoon lemon juice
- 1/2 cup pineapple ice cream topping
- 1 quart strawberry ice cream, softened
- 2 cups whipped topping
- 1/2 cup chopped walnuts, toasted
Chocolate syrup
- 8 maraschino cherries with stems

1 Pour chocolate topping into crust; freeze for 5 minutes or until chocolate is firm.

2 Meanwhile, place bananas in a small bowl; toss with lemon juice. Arrange bananas over chocolate topping. Layer with pineapple topping, ice cream, whipped topping and walnuts.

3 Cover and freeze until firm. Remove from the freezer 15 minutes before cutting. Garnish with chocolate syrup and cherries.

YIELD: 8 SERVINGS.

sweetheart surprise cupcakes

Margaret Wilson, Sun City, California

Kids really love the fruity surprise tucked inside these sweet and tender cupcakes.

- 1 package (18-1/4 ounces) strawberry cake mix
- 2 cups (16 ounces) sour cream
- 2 eggs
- 1/3 cup strawberry preserves
- 1 can (16 ounces) vanilla frosting, *divided*
Red food coloring
Red nonpareils and pink jimmies

1 In a large bowl, combine the cake mix, sour cream and eggs. Beat on low speed for 30 seconds; beat on medium for 2 minutes.

2 Place paper or foil liners in heart-shaped or standard muffin tins. (If using standard tins, tuck a 1/2-in. foil ball or marble between the liner and cup to form a heart shape.) Fill cups half full with batter. Using the end of a wooden spoon handle, make an indentation in the center of each; fill with 1/2 teaspoon preserves. Top with remaining batter.

3 Bake at 350° for 22-27 minutes or until a toothpick inserted in the cake portion comes out clean. Cool for 10 minutes before removing from pans to wire racks to cool completely.

4 Place a third of the frosting in a small bowl; tint pink with red food coloring. Frost cupcakes with white frosting; pipe edges with pink frosting. Decorate with nonpareils and jimmies.

YIELD: ABOUT 2 DOZEN.

upside-down turtle muffins

Patrice Bruwer, Lowell, Michigan

These gems feature an ooey-gooey caramel center and a glossy chocolate glaze topped with sweet pecans. They're perfect when you want something sweet.

1	cup all-purpose flour
1/4	cup chopped pecans
1	teaspoon baking soda
1/2	teaspoon salt
1/2	cup semisweet chocolate chips
3	tablespoons butter
1/3	cup packed brown sugar
1/3	cup buttermilk
1	egg, lightly beaten
1	teaspoon vanilla extract
16	Riesen chewy chocolate-covered caramels, *divided*
24	pecan halves

1 In a small bowl, combine the flour, chopped pecans, baking soda and salt; set aside. In a microwave-safe bowl, melt chocolate chips and butter; stir until smooth. Cool slightly. Stir in the brown sugar, buttermilk, egg and vanilla. Stir into dry ingredients just until moistened.

2 Fill greased muffin cups three-fourths full. Press one caramel into the center of each muffin cup. Bake at 400° for 12-14 minutes or until a toothpick inserted into the edge comes out clean.

3 Cool for 1 minute; invert onto a baking sheet. Top muffins with the remaining caramels; return to the oven for 1-2 minutes or until caramel is softened. Place three pecan halves on each muffin. Serve warm.

YIELD: 8 MUFFINS.

watermelon sherbet smoothies

(pictured at left)

Jamie Cockerel, Kalamazoo, Michigan

These fast-to-fix smoothies have become a summertime tradition for my sons. There's nothing quite as refreshing as these chilly drinks that beat the heat!

- 3 cups cubed seedless watermelon
- 1 cup crushed ice
- 1 cup watermelon, raspberry *or* lime sherbet
- 4 teaspoons lime juice
- 2 teaspoons miniature semisweet chocolate chips

In a blender, combine watermelon, ice, sherbet and lime juice; cover and process for 30 seconds or until smooth. Stir if necessary. Pour into chilled glasses; sprinkle with chocolate chips. Serve immediately.

YIELD: 4 SERVINGS.

cherry chocolate coconut cupcakes

Sandy Ploy, Whitefish Bay, Wisconsin

Chocolate-covered coconut candy is tucked inside each little cupcake. The creamy frosting is complemented by coarse sugar and chocolate-covered cherries.

- 1 package (10 to 12 ounces) vanilla *or* white chips
- 1/2 cup butter, cubed
- 1 cup heavy whipping cream
- 1 teaspoon coconut extract
- 1 can (21 ounces) cherry pie filling
- 1 cup buttermilk
- 2 eggs
- 2 cups all-purpose flour
- 2 cups sugar
- 3/4 cup baking cocoa
- 2 teaspoons baking soda
- 1 teaspoon baking powder
- 1/2 teaspoon salt
- 6 packages (1.9 ounces *each*) chocolate-covered coconut candy bars
- 1/2 cup semisweet chocolate chips
- 1 teaspoon shortening
- 24 maraschino cherries, well drained
- 3-1/4 cups confectioners' sugar
- 2 tablespoons coarse sugar

1 For ganache, place vanilla chips and butter in a large bowl. In a small saucepan, bring cream just to a boil. Pour over chip mixture; whisk until smooth. Stir in extract. Refrigerate for at least 4 hours, stirring occasionally.

2 In a large bowl, beat the pie filling, buttermilk and eggs until well blended. Combine the flour, sugar, cocoa, baking soda, baking powder and salt; gradually beat into pie filling mixture until blended.

3 Fill paper-lined muffin cups one-third full. Cut candy bars in half; place half of a candy bar in center of each cupcake. Cover each with 2 tablespoons batter.

4 Bake at 375° for 16-20 minutes or until a toothpick inserted near the center comes out clean. Cool for 10 minutes before removing from pans to wire racks to cool completely.

5 Meanwhile, in a microwave, melt chocolate chips and shortening; stir until smooth. Dip cherries in chocolate mixture; allow excess to drip off. Place on a waxed paper-lined baking sheet. Refrigerate until set.

6 Remove ganache from refrigerator; gradually beat in confectioners' sugar until frosting is light and fluffy. Pipe over cupcakes; sprinkle with coarse sugar. Garnish with chocolate-dipped cherries.

YIELD: 2 DOZEN.

icy blue parfaits

Taste of Home Test Kitchen

Kids of all ages will get a kick out of these stunning parfaits. They'll add a colorful touch to your next pool party or cookout.

- 1 package (3 ounces) cream cheese, softened
- 1 carton (8 ounces) frozen whipped topping, thawed
- 1 package (14 ounces) blue gelatin snack cups *or* 1-1/3 cups cubed blue gelatin
- 1 cup fresh *or* frozen blueberries

1 In a large bowl, beat cream cheese until smooth; beat in whipped topping. Unmold gelatin from snack cups; cut into 1/2-in. cubes.

2 In four parfait glasses or dessert bowls, layer half of the cream cheese mixture, gelatin and blueberries. Repeat layers. Chill until serving.

YIELD: 4 SERVINGS.

frosted butter cookies

Sharon Pickerd, Sparta, Michigan

These cookies melt in your mouth...even when they're not frosted. The recipe was handed down years ago from a cousin who tasted the cookies at a children's fundraiser.

- 2 cups butter, softened
- 1-3/4 cups sugar
- 1 egg yolk
- 4 cups all-purpose flour
- Prepared vanilla frosting
- Food coloring and decorating sprinkles, optional

1 In a large bowl, cream butter and sugar until light and fluffy. Beat in egg yolk. Gradually add flour and mix well.

2 Roll into 1-in. balls. Place 2 in. apart on ungreased baking sheets. Flatten with a glass dipped in flour. Bake at 375° for 8-10 minutes or until lightly browned. Remove to wire racks to cool.

3 Tint frosting with food coloring if desired. Frost cookies. Decorate as desired.

YIELD: 4-1/2 DOZEN.

makeover strawberry cake

Gail Long, Pelham, Alabama

My family just loves this wonderful and easy cake that's as pretty as it is tasty!

1 package (18-1/4 ounces) white cake mix
1 package (.3 ounce) sugar-free strawberry gelatin
4 egg whites
1/3 cup canola oil
1 cup frozen unsweetened strawberries, thawed
1/2 cup water

ICING:

1/3 cup butter, softened
2-1/3 cups confectioners' sugar

1 Line two 9-in. round baking pans with waxed paper. Coat pans with cooking spray and sprinkle with flour; set aside. In a large bowl, combine cake mix and gelatin. Add egg whites and oil; beat until well blended.

2 In a small bowl, mash strawberries in their juice. Set aside 3 tablespoons for icing. Add water and remaining berries to the batter; mix well.

3 Pour into prepared pans. Bake at 350° for 20-25 minutes or until a toothpick inserted near the center comes out clean. Cool for 10 minutes before removing from pans to wire racks to cool completely.

4 For icing, in a small bowl, combine butter and reserved strawberries. Gradually beat in confectioners' sugar until light and fluffy. Place one cake layer on a serving plate; top with half of the icing. Repeat layers.

YIELD: 16 SERVINGS.

chocolate chip dip

(pictured at left)

Heather Koenig, Prairie du Chien, Wisconsin

Is there a kid alive—or a kid at heart—who wouldn't gobble up this creamy dip for graham crackers? It beats dunking them in milk, hands down!

- 1 package (8 ounces) cream cheese, softened
- 1/2 cup butter, softened
- 3/4 cup confectioners' sugar
- 2 tablespoons brown sugar
- 1 teaspoon vanilla extract
- 1 cup (6 ounces) miniature semisweet chocolate chips

Graham cracker sticks

1 In a small bowl, beat cream cheese and butter until light and fluffy. Add the sugars and vanilla; beat until smooth. Stir in chocolate chips. Serve with graham cracker sticks.

YIELD: 2 CUPS.

peanut butter blur

Jody Keysor, Cadyville, New York

With just four ingredients and a blender, you can create this frosty, frothy drink that will cool you—and a friend—right down to your toes!

- 1-1/2 cups vanilla ice cream
- 12 miniature peanut butter cups
- 1/4 cup 2% milk
- 3 tablespoons creamy peanut butter

1 In a blender, combine all ingredients; cover and process for 1-2 minutes or until blended. Pour into chilled glasses; serve immediately.

YIELD: 2 SERVINGS.

best friend cupcakes

Taste of Home Test Kitchen

These adorable little pups are double the fun when served with edible "Scooby Snacks" graham crackers that look like real dog treats. Kids will get a kick out of the presentation.

- 1 can (16 ounces) vanilla frosting

Tan *or* yellow food coloring

Cupcakes of your choice

Milano cookies

Milk chocolate candy coating discs

Yellow and brown M&M's

- 1 tube (4-1/4 ounces) black decorating icing

1 Tint frosting light tan. Generously frost cupcakes; mounding slightly off-center for the nose. Add cookies for ears.

2 Add a candy coating disc and a yellow M&M for eyes; brown M&M for the nose. Pipe a dot of icing as each pupil. Pipe a mouth.

YIELD: 2 DOZEN.

party time
BIRTHDAY

BIRTHDAY PARTY

Celebrate the big day with a menu sure to please young party-goers. Choose from-scratch or shortcut burgers and dogs, add a fun salad and dip, and top it off with a gorgeous cake they'll remember!

circus cake

Taste of Home Test Kitchen

Ideal for a child's party, this whimsical cake steals the show with its cotton candy topping and cookie-laced sides.

- 1 package (18-1/4 ounces) white cake mix
- 1 can (16 ounces) vanilla frosting
- Nerds candies
- Miniature chocolate cream-filled chocolate sandwich cookies
- Frosted animal crackers
- Miniature marshmallows
- Cotton candy
- Lollipops

1 Prepare and bake cake according to package directions, using two greased 9-in. round baking pans. Cool for 10 minutes before removing from pans to wire racks to cool completely.

2 Spread frosting between layers and over top and sides of cake. Lightly press the Nerds, sandwich cookies and animal crackers onto sides of cake. Arrange marshmallows along top edge of cake. Just before serving, arrange cotton candy and lollipops on top of cake.

YIELD: 12 SERVINGS.

orange fluff salad

(pictured at left)

Stacey Meyer, Merced, California

My sister gave me this fluffy salad recipe that whips up in a jiffy. Unlike many gelatin recipes that need to set for hours, this one's ready to serve right away. It's perfect for unexpected company.

- 1 cup (8 ounces) sour cream
- 1 package (3 ounces) lemon gelatin
- 2 cans (11 ounces *each*) mandarin oranges, drained
- 1 can (21 ounces) pineapple tidbits, drained
- 1 carton (8 ounces) frozen whipped topping, thawed
- Pastel miniature marshmallows, optional

1 Place sour cream in a large bowl. Sprinkle with gelatin and stir until blended. Fold in the oranges, pineapple and whipped topping. Sprinkle with marshmallows if desired.

YIELD: 8 SERVINGS.

bacon cheeseburger buns

Marjorie Miller, Haven, Kansas

Here's a fun way to serve bacon cheeseburgers without all the fuss of assembling sandwiches to serve a big group. These convenient packets can be dipped into ketchup or barbecue sauce as you eat them.

- 2 packages (1/4 ounce *each*) active dry yeast
- 2/3 cup warm water (110° to 115°)
- 2/3 cup warm milk (110° to 115°)
- 1/4 cup sugar
- 1/4 cup shortening
- 2 eggs
- 2 teaspoons salt
- 4-1/2 to 5 cups all-purpose flour
- FILLING:
- 1 pound sliced bacon, diced
- 2 pounds ground beef
- 1 small onion, chopped
- 1-1/2 teaspoons salt
- 1/2 teaspoon pepper
- 1 pound process cheese (Velveeta), cubed
- 3 to 4 tablespoons butter, melted
- Ketchup *or* barbecue sauce, optional

1 In a large bowl, dissolve yeast in warm water. Add the milk, sugar, shortening, eggs, salt and 3-1/2 cups flour; beat until smooth. Stir in enough remaining flour to form a soft dough.

2 Turn onto a floured surface; knead until smooth and elastic, about 6-8 minutes. Place in a greased bowl, turning once to grease top. Cover and let rise in a warm place until doubled, about 1 hour.

3 Meanwhile, in a large skillet, cook bacon over medium heat until crisp. Using a slotted spoon, remove to paper towels. In a Dutch oven, cook the beef, onion, salt and pepper over medium heat until meat is no longer pink; drain. Add bacon and cheese; cook and stir until cheese is melted. Remove from the heat.

4 Punch dough down. Turn onto a lightly floured surface; divide into fourths. Roll each portion into a 12-in. x 8-in. rectangle; cut each into six squares. Place 1/4 cup meat mixture in the center of each square. Bring corners together in the center and pinch to seal.

5 Place 2 in. apart on greased baking sheets. Bake at 400° for 9-11 minutes or until lightly browned. Brush with butter. Serve warm with ketchup if desired.

YIELD: 2 DOZEN.

caterpillar cake

(pictured at right)

Lee Dean, Boaz, Alabama

This cute little caterpillar is easy to make with a boxed cake mix and prepared frosting. To save yet another step, tint the frosting and omit the coconut.

- 1 package (18-1/4 ounces) yellow cake mix
- 1 can (16 ounces) vanilla frosting
- 2-1/2 cups flaked coconut, *divided*
- 2 small purple gumdrops
- 1 small red gumdrop
- 2 small orange gumdrops
- 2 pretzel sticks

Yellow, red and green liquid food coloring

1 Prepare cake batter according to package directions. Fill a greased 8-oz. custard cup three-fourths full. Pour remaining batter into a greased 10-in. fluted tube pan.

2 Bake the custard cup at 350° for 20-25 minutes and the tube cake for 40-45 minutes or until a toothpick inserted near the center comes out clean. Cool for 10 minutes before removing cakes to wire racks to cool completely.

3 Cut large cake in half widthwise. To form caterpillar, place one half on a 15-in. x 10-in. covered board. Place the remaining portion next to the first to form an "S." With a serrated knife, level top and bottom of small cake; place on one end of caterpillar for head.

4 Frost the small cake with vanilla frosting; gently press 1/4 cup coconut into frosting. Add purple gumdrops for eyes. For mouth, flatten red gumdrop between waxed paper with a rolling pin; place below eyes. For antennae, press orange gumdrops onto pretzels; insert into head.

5 Place 3/4 cup coconut each in three small resealable plastic bags. Tint one orange with yellow and red food coloring; tint one green and one yellow. Frost the caterpillar with remaining vanilla frosting. Press alternate colors of coconut into frosting.

YIELD: 8-10 SERVINGS.

mini burgers with the works

Linda Lane, Bennington, Vermont

I started preparing these mini burgers several years ago as a way to use up bread crusts accumulating in my freezer. Their tiny size makes them simply irresistible.

- 1/4 pound ground beef
- 3 slices process American cheese
- 4 slices white bread (heels of loaf recommended)
- 2 tablespoons prepared Thousand Island salad dressing
- 2 pearl onions, thinly sliced
- 4 baby dill pickles, thinly sliced
- 3 cherry tomatoes, thinly sliced

1 Shape beef into twelve 1-in. patties. Place on a microwave-safe plate lined with paper towels. Cover with another paper towel; microwave on high for 1 minute or until meat is no longer pink. Cut each slice of cheese into fourths; set aside.

2 Using a 1-in. round cookie cutter, cut out six circles from each slice of bread. Spread half of the bread circles with dressing. Layer with burgers, cheese, onions, pickles and tomatoes. Top with remaining bread circles; secure with toothpicks.

YIELD: 1 DOZEN.

EDITOR'S NOTE: This recipe was tested in a 1,100-watt microwave.

play ball cake

Sue Gronholz, Beaver Dam, Wisconsin

You won't need fancy pans to make this sporting dessert. Our kids and their cousins all wanted pieces that had the red licorice lacing! Fresh, pliable licorice works the best for forming the laces on the curved ball cake.

1/2 cup shortening
1-1/2 cups sugar
2 eggs
1 teaspoon vanilla extract
2-1/2 cups cake flour
2 teaspoons baking powder
1/2 teaspoon salt
1 cup milk
FROSTING:
1/2 cup shortening
1/2 cup butter, softened
3 cups confectioners' sugar
4 tablespoons milk, *divided*
1/2 teaspoon vanilla extract
1/4 teaspoon almond extract
Dash salt
1/4 cup baking cocoa
Shoestring red licorice

1 In a large bowl, cream shortening and sugar until light and fluffy. Add eggs, one at a time, beating well after each addition. Beat in vanilla. Combine the flour, baking powder and salt; add alternately to creamed mixture with milk, beating well after each addition. Pour 1-1/2 cups batter into a greased and floured 3-cup ovenproof bowl.

2 Pour remaining batter into a greased and floured 9-in. round baking pan. Bake both cakes at 325° for 40-45 minutes or until a toothpick inserted near the center comes out clean. Cool for 10 minutes before removing to wire racks to cool completely.

3 For frosting, in a large bowl, beat the shortening, butter and confectioners' sugar until smooth. Beat in 3 tablespoons milk, extracts and salt until smooth. Set aside 1 cup.

4 To the remaining frosting, beat in cocoa and remaining milk. Cut a 3-in. x 1-in. oval for the thumb opening from an edge of the 9-in. cake. Place the cake on an 11-in. covered board and frost with chocolate frosting.

5 With four pieces of licorice, form two crosses over thumb opening for laces in mitt. Frost the rounded cake with white frosting. Use licorice pieces to form laces of ball. Place on mitt cake.

YIELD: 8-10 SERVINGS.

dogs in a sweater

Taste of Home Test Kitchen

For a new twist on an old favorite, try these skewered hot dogs wrapped with breadstick dough and baked. They're fun to dip in ketchup, mustard or ranch dressing.

- 1 tube (11 ounces) refrigerated breadsticks
- 12 Popsicle sticks
- 12 hot dogs

1 Separate breadstick dough; roll each piece into a 15-in. rope. Insert a Popsicle stick into each hot dog lengthwise. Starting at one end, wrap dough in a spiral around hot dog; pinch ends to seal. Place 1 in. apart on a baking sheet coated with cooking spray. Bake at 350° for 18-20 minutes or until golden brown.

YIELD: 12 SERVINGS.

indiana-style corn dogs

Sally Denney, Warsaw, Indiana

Among the best parts of the many fairs and festivals in Indiana are the corn dogs served there! My family adores corn dogs, so I make them fairly often at home.

- 1/2 cup yellow cornmeal
- 1 cup all-purpose flour
- 1 tablespoon baking powder
- 1 teaspoon salt
- 1 tablespoon sugar
- 1 cup evaporated milk
- 1 egg, lightly beaten

- 1/4 teaspoon paprika
- 1/2 teaspoon ground mustard

Dash of pepper

- 10 to 16 hot dogs

Oil for deep-fat frying

1 In large bowl, mix the first 10 ingredients. Pour mixture into a tall glass.

2 Skewer hot dogs with wooden skewers; dip in mixture. Deep-fry at 375° until golden brown (about 2 minutes). Drain on paper towels.

YIELD: 10-16 CORN DOGS.

mozzarella dip

Faye Hintz, Springfield, Missouri

For a creamy, cheesy dip that inspires munching on raw vegetables, give this recipe a try. It's a great party snack.

- 2 cups mayonnaise
- 1 cup (8 ounces) sour cream
- 1 cup (4 ounces) shredded mozzarella cheese
- 2 tablespoons grated Parmesan cheese
- 1 tablespoon dried minced onion
- 1 teaspoon sugar

Dash *each* garlic salt and seasoned salt

1 In a large bowl, combine all ingredients. Cover and chill for at least 1 hour. Serve with raw vegetables or tortilla chips.

YIELD: 3-1/2 CUPS.

party time
HALLOWEEN

HALLOWEEN

Thrill your goblins with bewitching culinary delights! Have some spooky fun, or introduce youngsters to beloved classics like homemade popcorn balls and caramel apples.

yummy mummy with veggie dip

Heather Snow, Salt Lake City, Utah

I came up with this idea for dressing up a veggie tray for our annual Halloween party, and everyone got wrapped up in it! Frozen bread dough and dip mix make this a simple and easy appetizer that's as much fun to display as it is to eat.

1 loaf (1 pound) frozen bread dough, thawed
3 pieces string cheese
2 cups (16 ounces) sour cream
1 envelope fiesta ranch dip mix
1 pitted ripe olive
Assorted crackers and fresh vegetables

1 Let dough rise according to package directions. Place it on a greased baking sheet. For mummy, roll out dough into a 12-in. oval that is more narrow at the bottom. For the neck, make an indentation on each side, about 1 in. down from the top. Let rise in a warm place for 20 minutes.

2 Bake at 350° for 20-25 minutes or until golden brown. Arrange strips of string cheese over bread; bake 1-2 minutes longer or until cheese is melted. Remove from pan to a wire rack to cool.

3 Meanwhile, in a small bowl, combine sour cream and dip mix. Chill until serving.

4 Cut mummy in half horizontally. Hollow out bottom half, leaving a 3/4-in. shell. Cut removed bread into cubes; set aside. Place bread bottom on a serving plate. Spoon dip into shell. Replace top. For eyes, cut olive and position on head. Serve with crackers, vegetables and reserved bread.

YIELD: 16 SERVINGS (2 CUPS DIP).

carnival caramel apples

(pictured at left)

Gail Prather, Bethel, Minnesota

With four kids (one whose birthday is November 1), we celebrate Halloween in style at our house. These caramel apples are a tried-and-true favorite year after year.

- 1/2 cup butter, cubed
- 2 cups packed brown sugar
- 1 cup light corn syrup
- Dash salt
- 1 can (14 ounces) sweetened condensed milk
- 1 teaspoon vanilla extract
- 10 to 12 Popsicle sticks
- 10 to 12 medium tart apples, washed and dried
- 1 cup salted peanuts, chopped

1 In a large heavy saucepan, melt butter; add the brown sugar, corn syrup and salt. Cook and stir over medium heat until mixture comes to a boil, about 10-12 minutes. Stir in milk. Cook and stir until a candy thermometer reads 248° (firm-ball stage). Remove from the heat; stir in vanilla.

2 Insert Popsicle sticks into apples. Dip apples into hot caramel mixture; turn to coat. Dip bottoms into peanuts. Let stand on greased waxed paper until set.

YIELD: 10-12 APPLES.

EDITOR'S NOTE: We recommend that you test your candy thermometer before each use by bringing water to a boil; the thermometer should read 212°. Adjust your recipe temperature up or down based on your test.

spiced apple-grape juice

Claire Beattie, Toronto, Ontario

This warm spiced drink will be the life of the party. It's also nice to just cozy up with at home on a chilly fall night.

- 4 cups white grape juice
- 3 cups unsweetened apple juice
- 1 cup water
- 2 cinnamon sticks (3 inches)
- 12 whole cloves
- 8 whole allspice

1 In a large saucepan, combine the grape juice, apple juice and water. Place the spices on a double thickness of cheesecloth; bring up corners of cloth and tie with string to form a bag. Add to the pan. Bring to a boil. Reduce heat; simmer, uncovered, for 1 to 1-1/2 hours or until flavors are blended. Discard spice bag. Serve warm in mugs.

YIELD: 8 SERVINGS.

pumpkin pie dip

Laurie LaClair, North Richland Hills, Texas

I came up with this rich, creamy dip when I had a small amount of canned pumpkin left in the fridge after my holiday baking. It is also great served with sliced pears and apples, as a spread on zucchini bread or atop any other nut bread.

- 1 package (8 ounces) cream cheese, softened
- 2 cups confectioners' sugar
- 1 cup canned pumpkin
- 1/2 cup sour cream
- 1 teaspoon ground cinnamon
- 1 teaspoon pumpkin pie spice
- 1/2 teaspoon ground ginger
- Gingersnap cookies

1 In a large bowl, beat cream cheese and confectioners' sugar until smooth. Beat in the pumpkin, sour cream, cinnamon, pie spice and ginger until blended. Serve with gingersnaps.

YIELD: 4 CUPS.

jack-o'-lantern turnovers

Marge Free, Brandon, Mississippi

I carved these clever pumpkin pastries to feed my hungry bunch at Halloween. The ground beef filling has a hint of onion and mustard.

1/2	pound ground beef
1	tablespoon finely chopped onion
4	ounces cubed part-skim mozzarella cheese
1/4	cup prepared mustard
2	tubes (16.3 ounces *each*) large refrigerated flaky biscuits
1	egg, lightly beaten

1 In a large skillet, cook beef and onion over medium heat until meat is no longer pink; drain. Add cheese and mustard; cook and stir until cheese is melted. Cool slightly.

2 Flatten each biscuit into a 4-in. circle; place four biscuits in each of two greased 15-in. x 10-in. x 1-in. baking pans. Spoon 2 heaping tablespoons of meat mixture onto each.

3 Using a sharp knife or cookie cutters, cut out jack-o'-lantern faces from remaining biscuit circles; place over meat mixture and pinch edges to seal tightly. Re-roll scraps if desired and cut out stems for pumpkins.

4 Brush with egg. Bake at 350° for 10-15 minutes or until golden brown.

YIELD: 8 SERVINGS.

witch's crispy hat

(pictured at right)

Taste of Home Test Kitchen

You won't want to keep this clever recipe under your hat! Our chocolate-covered crispy treat will appeal to kids of all ages.

8	cups miniature marshmallows
1/2	cup butter, cubed
12	cups crisp rice cereal
3-1/3	cups confectioners' sugar
1-1/2	cups heavy whipping cream
8	ounces unsweetened chocolate, chopped
4	teaspoons vanilla extract
3/4	cup butter, softened
1	ice cream sugar cone
4	sour apple Laffy Taffy candies
4	grape Laffy Taffy candies

1 In a Dutch oven, combine marshmallows and butter. Cook and stir over medium-low heat until melted and blended. Remove from the heat; stir in cereal. Press 4 cups into a greased 9-in. round pan and remaining mixture into a greased 15-in. x 10-in. x 1-in. pan; cool.

2 In a large saucepan, bring the confectioners' sugar and cream to a boil, stirring constantly. Remove from the heat; stir in chocolate until melted and smooth. Stir in vanilla. Cool until mixture is thickened, about 25 minutes, stirring occasionally.

3 For frosting, in a large bowl, cream butter until light and fluffy. Gradually beat in chocolate mixture until blended. Refrigerate up to 30 minutes.

4 To assemble hat, cut six circles out of cereal mixture in the 15-in. x 10-in. pan using 5-1/2-in., 5-in., 4-1/2-in., 4-in., 3-in. and 2-in. round cookie cutters (save remaining mixture for another use).

5 Remove cereal mixture from 9-in. pan and place on a serving platter. Top with remaining circles, stacking from large to small. Top with sugar cone. Spread with frosting.

6 Unwrap and microwave apple candies on high for 10-20 seconds or until softened. Roll out to 1/8-in. thickness; cut with a star-shaped cookie cutter. Repeat with grape candies; cut into moon shapes. Press moons and stars onto hat.

YIELD: 1 WITCH'S HAT (30 SERVINGS).

trick-or-treat nachos

(pictured at left)

Taste of Home Test Kitchen

Here's a great snack that will fill the kids' bellies before they head out to collect candy. To maintain the shape of the cutouts, spread the bean mixture with a butter knife or thin spatula. You can use any shape of cookie cutter that you have on hand.

20 corn tortillas (6 inches)
Nonstick cooking spray
1 garlic clove, minced
1 tablespoon olive oil
1 cup refried beans
3 tablespoons salsa
1/2 teaspoon ground cumin
1/4 cup minced fresh cilantro
1-1/4 cups shredded cheddar cheese
Pimiento-stuffed olives, sliced ripe olives, green pepper strips and green onions

1 Using 3-in. Halloween-shaped cookie cutters, cut out one shape from each tortilla. Place on baking sheets coated with cooking spray. Spritz cutouts with cooking spray. Bake at 350° for 8-10 minutes or until crisp.

2 Meanwhile, in a saucepan, saute garlic in oil for 1 minute. Add beans, salsa and cumin; heat through.

3 Stir in cilantro. Spread 1 tablespoonful bean mixture on each cutout; top each with 1 tablespoon cheese. Bake for 3 minutes or cheese is melted. Decorate with olives, green pepper and onions.

YIELD: 20 NACHOS.

old-time popcorn balls

LaReine Stevens, Ypsilanti, Michigan

These old-time popcorn balls are great anytime, but they're especially fun to pass out to trick-or-treaters or to use as spooky party favors! They always look appealing when covered in a clear wrap and tied with festive ribbon.

2 quarts popped popcorn
1/2 cup molasses
1/2 cup sugar
1/3 cup water
1 tablespoon white vinegar
1 tablespoon butter
1/4 teaspoon baking soda

1 Place popcorn in a large bowl and set aside. In a large heavy saucepan, combine the molasses, sugar, water, vinegar and butter. Cook, without stirring, over medium heat until the mixture reaches 235° on a candy thermometer (soft-ball stage). Add baking soda and stir well.

2 Immediately pour over popcorn, stirring with a wooden spoon until coated. When cool enough to handle, quickly shape into 3-in. balls, dipping hands in cool water to prevent the syrup from sticking.

YIELD: 6-8 SERVINGS.

EDITOR'S NOTE: We recommend that you test your candy thermometer before each use by bringing water to a boil; the thermometer should read 212°. Adjust your recipe temperature up or down based on your test.

gruesome green toes

Jamey Jackson, Gile, Wisconsin

This cookie will have you in and out of the kitchen in no time. Children will have fun attaching the candy toenails!

12 ounces white candy coating, coarsely chopped
Green paste food coloring
22 peanut butter cream-filled sandwich cookies
11 Crows candies, halved lengthwise

1 In a microwave, melt candy coating; stir until smooth. Tint green. Dip one cookie into candy coating. Let excess drip off and place on waxed paper. Immediately place a candy half, cut side down, on the cookie. Repeat. Let stand for 15 minutes or until set.

YIELD: 22 COOKIES.

dracula cookies

(pictured at right)

Christy Hinrichs, Parkville, Missouri

Come late October, our friends and family can count on me to re-introduce them to my darling Dracula cookies!

- 6 hazelnut truffles
- 5 ounces white candy coating, chopped
- 1 green *or* red Fruit Roll-Up
- 6 cream-filled chocolate sandwich cookies
- 1 can (6.4 ounces) black decorating icing
- 6 slivered almonds, cut in half

1 Place truffles on a waxed paper-lined pan. Freeze for 10 minutes or until chilled. Meanwhile, in a microwave-safe bowl, melt candy coating; stir until smooth. Dip truffles in coating to cover completely; allow excess to drip off. Return to prepared pan. Refrigerate until hardened.

2 Cut Fruit Roll-Up into 2-1/2-in. x 1-1/2-in. strips. Reheat candy coating if necessary. Dip truffles in candy coating again; allow excess to drip off. Place one on each cookie. Wrap a fruit strip around base of truffle for cape. Allow to set.

3 Using decorating icing and a round tip, pipe hair, eyes and mouth on each. Insert almonds for fangs.

YIELD: 6 COOKIES.

EDITOR'S NOTE: This recipe was tested with Ferrero Rocher hazelnut truffles.

gummy worm punch

Kathy Kittell, Lenexa, Kansas

We thought this punch would be such fun for Halloween that we garnished it with a chilling gummy-worm ice ring! To prepare it for other types of parties, simply eliminate the gummy worms.

- 4 cups unsweetened apple juice
- 4 cups orange juice
- 2/3 cup thawed lemonade concentrate
- 2 cups water
- 20 gummy worms
- 4 cups lemon-lime soda, chilled

1 In a punch bowl, combine the apple juice, orange juice and lemonade concentrate. Pour water and 1 cup juice mixture into a 5-cup ring mold; add gummy worms. Freeze until solid. Meanwhile, refrigerate juice mixture until chilled.

2 Just before serving, add soda to juice mixture. Unmold ice ring by wrapping the bottom of the mold in a damp hot dishcloth; invert onto a baking sheet. Place worm side up in punch bowl.

YIELD: 3 QUARTS.

presto pumpkin seeds

Taste of Home Test Kitchen

These easy, crunchy seeds are perfect for those busy sewing costumes or planning parties.

- 1/2 cup fresh pumpkin seeds
- 1/8 teaspoon salt

1 In a bowl, toss pumpkin seeds with salt. Spread in a single layer on a microwave-safe plate. Microwave, uncovered, on high for 2-3 minutes or until seeds are crunchy and lightly browned, stirring each minute.

YIELD: 1/2 CUP.

party time
WINTER FUN

WINTER FUN

Cure your little one's cabin fever with a delightful celebration of the coldest season. Learn, cook and play together. Warm up with a fanciful combo of grilled cheese, tomato soup and more.

snowflake tomato soup

Taste of Home Test Kitchen

Our sensational soup packs lots of pleasing ingredients. It's extra fun to eat when it's decorated with a pretty snowflake.

- 2 cans (28 ounces *each*) crushed tomatoes
- 1 can (14-1/2 ounces) chicken broth
- 2 tablespoons minced fresh oregano *or* 2 teaspoons dried oregano
- 1 to 2 tablespoons sugar
- 1 cup heavy whipping cream
- 1/3 cup sour cream

1 In a blender, process tomatoes, one can at a time, until smooth. Transfer to a large saucepan. Stir in the broth; bring to a boil. Reduce heat; cover and simmer for 10 minutes. Stir in the oregano and sugar. Add a small amount of hot tomato mixture to whipping cream; return all to the saucepan. Cook until slightly thickened (do not boil).

2 Cut a small hole in the corner of a pastry or plastic bag; fill with sour cream. Pipe a snowflake on each bowl of soup.

YIELD: 8-10 SERVINGS.

hot cocoa

Vicki Holloway, Joelton, Tennessee

Treat family and friends to this rich homemade cocoa.
It will warm even the coldest winter's chill!

  1   cup sugar
2/3   cup baking cocoa
1/4   teaspoon salt
  8   cups 2% milk
2/3   cup water
  2   teaspoons vanilla extract
1/2   teaspoon almond extract
Miniature marshmallows, optional

1 In a large saucepan, combine the sugar, cocoa
   and salt. Stir in milk and water. Cook and stir
   over medium heat until heated through. Remove
   from the heat; stir in extracts. Serve in mugs with
   marshmallows if desired.

YIELD: 10 SERVINGS (2-1/2 QUARTS).

winter warm-up!

Treat your children and their
friends to a make-your-own
hot chocolate bar. They'll love
getting creative with these
stir-ins and toppings:

- Mini marshmallows
- Cinnamon
- Whipped cream
- Chocolate chips
- Sprinkles and jimmies
- Colored sugar
- Crushed candy canes

alpine cheese melts

Taste of Home Test Kitchen

Make grilled cheese sandwiches festive with cute winter-themed cutters like pine trees or mittens. Try these with whole wheat bread and sourdough if it better suits your gang's tastes.

18   slices white bread
18   slices pumpernickel bread
3   cups (12 ounces) shredded Colby-Monterey Jack cheese
1   cup plus 2 tablespoons mayonnaise
1/3   cup chopped green onions
1-1/2 teaspoons minced fresh basil *or* 1/2 teaspoon dried basil
1/4   to 1/2 teaspoon garlic powder
Butter, softened

1   Using a 3-1/2-in. cookie cutter, cut a shape in the center of each slice of bread; remove cutouts. Place a white bread cutout in each slice of pumpernickel. Place a pumpernickel cutout in each slice of white bread.

2   In a large bowl, combine the cheese, mayonnaise, onions, basil and garlic powder. Spread over nine slices of bread; top with remaining bread. Butter outsides of sandwiches.

3   In a large skillet over medium heat, toast sandwiches on each side until bread is golden brown and cheese is melted.

YIELD: 9 SANDWICHES.

festive apple dip

Theresa Tometich, Coralville, Iowa

I came up with this layered peanut butter treat when my dad gave me a big bag of apples. In addition to serving it with apples, try it with graham crackers, vanilla wafers, banana chunks or animal crackers.

1   package (8 ounces) cream cheese, softened
1/2   cup creamy peanut butter
1/3   cup packed brown sugar
1   teaspoon vanilla extract
1/2   cup miniature marshmallows
1   jar (11-3/4 ounces) hot fudge ice cream topping
2   tablespoons chopped mixed nuts *or* chopped peanuts
3   *each* medium red and green apples, cut into wedges
2   tablespoons lemon juice

1   In a small bowl, beat the cream cheese, peanut butter, brown sugar and vanilla until smooth; stir in marshmallows.

2   Spoon half into a 3-cup bowl; spread with half of the hot fudge topping. Repeat layers. Sprinkle with nuts. Toss the apples with lemon juice. Serve immediately with dip.

YIELD: ABOUT 8 SERVINGS.

4 With well-greased hands, spread marshmallow mixture into the prepared pan. Sprinkle 2 tablespoons of confectioners' sugar over the top. Cover mixture and let stand at room temperature for 6 hours or overnight.

5 Cut 15 snowflakes with a greased 2-1/2-in. snowflake-shaped cookie cutter; toss in remaining confectioners' sugar. Gently press lollipop stick into each snowflake. Store in an airtight container in a cool dry place.

YIELD: 15 POPS.

EDITOR'S NOTE: We recommend that you test your candy thermometer before each use by bringing water to a boil; the thermometer should read 212°. Adjust your recipe temperature up or down based on your test.

marshmallow pops

Jennifer Andrzejewski, Grizzly Flats, California

Homemade marshmallows are fun to eat on a stick or to stir in your favorite hot chocolate. Their melt-in-your-mouth texture appeals to the young and the young at heart.

1/2 cup cold water
3 envelopes unflavored gelatin
2 cups sugar
1 cup light corn syrup
1/2 cup water
1/4 teaspoon salt
1 teaspoon almond extract
1/2 cup confectioners' sugar, *divided*
Lollipop sticks

1 In a large bowl, combine cold water and gelatin; set aside.

2 Meanwhile, in a large heavy saucepan over medium heat, combine the sugar, corn syrup, water and salt. Bring to a boil, stirring occasionally. Cover and cook for 2 minutes to dissolve sugar crystals; uncover and cook on medium-high heat, without stirring, until a candy thermometer reads 240° (soft-ball stage).

3 Remove from the heat and gradually add to gelatin. Beat on medium speed for 14 minutes. Add extract; beat 1 minute longer. Sprinkle 2 tablespoons confectioners' sugar into greased 13-in. x 9-in. pan.

sweet & salty snowmen

(pictured at right)

Carol Berndt, Avon, South Dakota

Kids have a blast creating different looks for their pretzel snowmen with candy scarves, buttons and top hats. If any are left over, they make cool table decorations posed in a glass filled with coconut snow. You can prop them with a bit of Styrofoam, too.

8 pretzel rods
6 ounces white baking chocolate, melted
Assorted candies: M&M's miniature baking bits, miniature chocolate chips, Chuckles jelly rings, small gumdrops, Fruit by the Foot fruit rolls

1 Dip pretzel rods two-thirds of the way into melted white chocolate, or drizzle chocolate over pretzels with a spoon. Attach baking bits for buttons and noses and chocolate chips for eyes.

2 For hat brims, add jelly rings to tops of pretzels. Dip the bottom of a small gumdrop into chocolate and press onto the tops for crowns of hats.

3 Carefully stand snowmen by placing them upright in a tall glass or pressing the bottom of the pretzel rods into a 2-in.-thick piece of Styrofoam.

4 For scarves, cut fruit rolls into thin strips; tie around snowmen.

YIELD: 8 SNOWMEN.

polar bear pie

Taste of Home Test Kitchen

Kids will warm up to this cool confection in a hurry! Since the treat is so simple to prepare, you'll easily be able to take your next party to another level of winter wonder.

3/4 cup butter, softened
1/2 cup sugar
1/2 teaspoon vanilla extract
1-1/4 cups all-purpose flour
3/4 cup ground almonds
1/4 teaspoon salt
4 cups blue moon ice cream, softened
ICING:
4-1/2 teaspoons meringue powder
2 cups confectioners' sugar
3 tablespoons water
Assorted gel *or* liquid food coloring
1 peppermint stick
1-1/4 cups whipped topping

1 In a small bowl, cream butter and sugar until light and fluffy. Beat in vanilla. Combine the flour, almonds and salt; gradually add to the creamed mixture and mix well. Cover and refrigerate for 2 hours or until easy to handle.

2 Press 1 cup dough onto the bottom of a greased 9-in. pie plate. Bake at 350° for 15-18 minutes or until edges are golden brown. Cool completely.

3 On a lightly floured surface, roll out remaining dough to 1/4-in. thickness. Cut out one 2-in. x 1-1/4-in. rectangle for sign. Using a 4-in. bear cookie cutter, cut out three bears.

4 Bake at 350° for 8-12 minutes or until edges are lightly browned. Cool for 2 minutes before removing to a wire rack to cool completely. Save dough scraps for another use. Spread ice cream into cooled crust; cover and freeze until set.

5 In a large bowl, beat the meringue powder, confectioners' sugar and water for 7-10 minutes or until thickened. Frost bears and sign; set aside to dry.

6 Using a new, unused fine paintbrush or a toothpick, paint eyes, nose and scarf on each bear with food coloring. Paint "North Pole" on sign; attach to peppermint stick with icing. Let dry.

7 Remove pie from freezer 15 minutes before serving. For icebergs, place one small and three large dollops of whipped topping on pie. Just before serving, insert bears into topping. Insert sign into ice cream.

YIELD: 8-10 servings.

EDITOR'S NOTE: As a substitute for blue moon ice cream, tint softened vanilla ice cream with blue food coloring. Meringue powder is available from Wilton Industries. Call 800-794-5866 or visit wilton.com.

mozzarella sticks

Mary Merchant, Barre, Vermont

I'm fond of these tasty snacks because they're baked, not fried. Little hands will clamor for them!

 3 tablespoons all-purpose flour
 2 eggs
 1 tablespoon water
 1 cup dry bread crumbs
2-1/2 teaspoons Italian seasoning
1/2 teaspoon garlic powder
1/8 teaspoon pepper
 12 sticks string cheese
 1 tablespoon butter, melted
 1 cup marinara or spaghetti sauce, heated

1 Place flour in a shallow bowl. In another bowl, beat eggs and water. In a third bowl, combine bread crumbs and seasonings. Coat cheese sticks with flour, then dip in egg mixture and coat with crumbs. Repeat egg and bread crumb coatings. Cover and chill for at least 4 hours or overnight.

2 Place on an ungreased baking sheet; drizzle with butter. Bake at 400° for 6-8 minutes or until heated through. Allow to stand for 3-5 minutes before serving. Serve with marinara for dipping.

YIELD: 4-6 SERVINGS.

EDITOR'S NOTE: Mozzarella cheese, cut into 4-in. x 1/2-in. sticks, can be substituted for the string cheese.

pineapple strawberry punch

Heather Dollins, Poplar Bluff, Missouri

For us, this drink has always been a must for special occasions. It's fruity and fun.

 2 packages (10 ounces each) frozen sweetened sliced strawberries, thawed
 1 can (46 ounces) pineapple juice, chilled
 4 cups lemon-lime soda, chilled

1 In a food processor, puree strawberries. Pour into a punch bowl. Stir in the juice and soda. Serve immediately.

YIELD: 12 SERVINGS (3 QUARTS).

Keep kids energized through the long winter months with party activities like these:

- Building snowmen or snow forts
- Sledding
- Skating
- Making gifts, crafts or ornaments
- A cooking lesson for Boy Scouts, Girl Scouts, 4-H or other groups

party time
SLUMBER PARTY

SLUMBER PARTY

Girls will have the energy to stay up all night after a fun buffet-style dinner of all things pizza! The next morning, treat them to a refreshing spritzer, yogurt parfaits and the most indulgent pancakes they've ever tasted!

pepperoni party dip

Donna Cajski, Milwaukee, Wisconsin

This rich pizza-flavored dip is loaded with tasty toppings like pepperoni, mushrooms and olives, and it's so easy to make in the microwave.

- 1 package (8 ounces) cream cheese, softened
- 1 can (4-1/4 ounces) chopped ripe olives, drained
- 1 can (4 ounces) mushroom stems and pieces, drained and chopped
- 1/3 cup chopped onion
- 24 slices pepperoni, chopped
- 1 can (8 ounces) pizza sauce
- 1 cup (4 ounces) shredded part-skim mozzarella cheese

Assorted crackers

1 Spread the cream cheese into an ungreased 9-in. microwave-safe pie plate. Top with olives, mushrooms, onion, pepperoni, pizza sauce and cheese.

2 Microwave, uncovered, at 70% power for 7-10 minutes or until heated through and cheese is melted. Serve with crackers.

YIELD: 8-10 SERVINGS.

EDITOR'S NOTE: This recipe was tested in a 1,100-watt microwave.

fruit pizza

Doris Sather, Strum, Wisconsin

This delicious recipe is nice to serve to company because it is so colorful and pretty. It's a wonderful use of fresh seasonal fruit.

CRUST:
- 1/2 cup butter, softened
- 1/2 cup shortening
- 1 cup sugar
- 1 egg
- 1 teaspoon vanilla extract
- 2 cups all-purpose flour
- 1/2 teaspoon cream of tartar
- 1/2 teaspoon baking soda
- 1/4 teaspoon salt

CREAM FILLING:
- 2 packages (8 ounces *each*) cream cheese, softened
- 1 cup confectioners' sugar
- 1 carton (8 ounces) frozen whipped topping, thawed

TOPPINGS:
- 2 tablespoons cornstarch
- 1 cup pineapple juice
- 1 cup orange juice
- 1-1/2 cups fresh raspberries
- 2 kiwifruit, peeled and sliced
- 2 medium bananas, sliced
- 1 pint fresh strawberries, hulled and sliced

1 In a small bowl, cream the butter, shortening and sugar until light and fluffy. Add egg and vanilla. Combine dry ingredients; gradually add to creamed mixture. Press dough into a 14- or 16-in. pizza pan. Bake at 350° 8-10 minutes or until light golden brown. Cool.

2 For filling, beat cream cheese until smooth; add sugar and whipped topping. Spread over crust.

3 For glaze, in a small saucepan, combine cornstarch and juices until smooth. Bring to a boil. Cook and stir for 1-2 minutes or until thickened. Set aside 1/2 cup; spread remaining warm glaze over filling.

4 Arrange fruit over pizza; brush with reserved glaze. Chill until serving. (Note: If making a day ahead, substitute another seasonal fruit for bananas.)

YIELD: 12 SERVINGS.

sausage pizza cups

Suzanne McKinley, Lyons, Georgia

My girls frequently have friends overnight, so I fix these quick mini pizzas often. Even their big brother likes them!

- 1 pound spicy *or* mild pork sausage
- 1 jar (14 ounces) pizza sauce
- 2 tablespoons ketchup
- 1/4 teaspoon garlic powder
- 2 tubes (10 ounces *each*) refrigerated biscuits

Shredded part-skim mozzarella cheese
Grated Parmesan cheese

1 In a large skillet, cook sausage over medium heat until no longer pink; drain. Stir in the pizza sauce, ketchup and garlic powder; set aside.

2 Press biscuits into 20 well-greased muffin cups. Spoon 1 or 2 tablespoons of the meat sauce into each biscuit; top with mozzarella cheese and sprinkle with Parmesan cheese.

3 Bake at 350° for 10 to 15 minutes or until golden brown. (Refrigerate or freeze any remaining meat sauce.)

YIELD: 20 PIZZA CUPS.

mama-mia meatballs

Karen Mellinger Baker, Dover, Ohio

I blend a can of crushed pineapple into my meatballs to create a taste-tempting treat. Best of all, the sweet and tangy glaze that coats these bite-size snacks is a snap to prepare.

- 1 can (8 ounces) crushed pineapple
- 1 egg
- 1/4 cup dry bread crumbs
- 1/8 teaspoon pepper
- 1/2 pound bulk pork sausage
- 1/2 pound ground beef

GLAZE:

- 1/4 cup packed brown sugar
- 1/4 cup ketchup
- 1/4 cup white vinegar
- 1/4 cup water
- 2 tablespoons Dijon-mayonnaise blend

1 Drain pineapple, reserving juice. Place pineapple and 2 tablespoons juice in a large bowl (set the remaining juice aside for glaze). Add the egg, bread crumbs and pepper to pineapple. Crumble sausage and beef over mixture and mix well. Shape into 1-in. balls.

2 Place meatballs on a greased rack in a shallow baking pan. Bake, uncovered, at 450° for 12-15 minutes or until no longer pink; drain.

3 Meanwhile, in a large skillet, combine glaze ingredients and reserved pineapple juice. Add meatballs. Bring to a boil over medium heat. Reduce heat; cook and stir for 5-10 minutes or until heated through.

YIELD: 2 DOZEN.

pizzeria salad

(pictured at right)

Taste of Home Cooking School

If your family loves pizza, let it inspire you to make a tempting salad!

- 2 prebaked mini pizza crusts
- 1/2 cup Western, Catalina *or* French salad dressing
- 1 tablespoon minced fresh basil *or* oregano
- 1 package (10 ounces) torn romaine lettuce (8 cups)
- 1 cup sliced pepperoni *or* chopped Canadian bacon
- 1 cup (4 ounces) shredded part-skim mozzarella cheese *or* cheese blend
- 1 can (2-1/4 ounces) sliced ripe olives, drained

1 Bake pizza crusts at 400° for 8-10 minutes or grill over medium heat until desired crispness. When cool enough to handle, tear into bite-size pieces; set aside.

2 In a small bowl, combine the salad dressing and basil; set aside. In a salad bowl, combine the lettuce, bread shell pieces, pepperoni, cheese and olives. Toss to mix ingredients. Drizzle each serving with dressing.

YIELD: 4 MAIN-DISH SERVINGS; 8 SIDE SALADS.

slumber party pancakes

(pictured at left)

Diane Hixon, Niceville, Florida

These fun chocolate pancakes disappear fast when the kids have friends over for a slumber party.

1/2	cup pancake mix
2	tablespoons baking cocoa
1	tablespoon sugar
1	egg
1/3	cup milk
1	tablespoon canola oil
1/4	cup miniature marshmallows
1/4	cup chopped pecans

Vanilla ice cream
Chocolate syrup *or* ice cream topping
Additional chopped pecans, optional

1 In a large bowl, combine pancake mix, cocoa and sugar. In another bowl, beat egg, milk and oil; stir into dry ingredients until almost smooth. Stir in marshmallows and pecans.

2 Pour batter by 1/4 cupfuls onto a lightly greased hot griddle; turn when bubbles form on top of pancakes. Cook until second side is golden brown. Top with ice cream and syrup. Sprinkle with pecans if desired.

YIELD: 4 SERVINGS.

EDITOR'S NOTE: This recipe may be prepared with Pancake Mix in a Jar (page 241) if desired.

strawberry banana spritzer

Karen Ann Bland, Gove, Kansas

This breakfast drink is smooth and refreshing, and not too sweet or heavy. Sparkling club soda makes it feel special.

6	cups orange juice
2	containers (10 ounces *each*) frozen sweetened sliced strawberries, partially thawed
2	medium ripe bananas, cut into chunks
3	cups club soda

1 In a blender, combine the orange juice, strawberries and bananas in batches until smooth. Transfer to a large pitcher. Refrigerate until serving. Just before serving, add club soda.

YIELD: 12 SERVINGS (3 QUARTS).

berry yogurt cups

Shannon Mink, Columbus, Ohio

Blueberries and strawberries jazz up yogurt in this perfect-for-summer yogurt parfait. Try using other fruit, like raspberries, banana and kiwi.

1-1/2	cups sliced fresh strawberries
1-1/2	cups fresh blueberries
3/4	cup (6 ounces) vanilla yogurt
1	teaspoon sugar
1/8	to 1/4 teaspoon ground cinnamon

1 Divide the strawberries and blueberries among four individual serving dishes. In a small bowl, combine the yogurt, sugar and cinnamon; spoon over fruit.

YIELD: 4 SERVINGS.

yummy tummy
(FOR LITTLE COOKS)

hot spiced cider

Trinda Heinrich, Lakemoor, Illinois

It's such a treat to come to come home to this warm, comforting cider after a day of playing in the snow. This is a nice change from hot chocolate.

2-1/2 cups apple cider *or* unsweetened apple juice
2/3 cup orange juice
1/3 cup sugar
2   tablespoons lemon juice
1/4 teaspoon ground nutmeg
1   cinnamon stick (3 inches)
12   whole cloves

1 In a 1-1/2-qt. slow cooker, combine the first five ingredients. Place cinnamon stick and cloves on a double thickness of cheesecloth; bring up corners of cloth and tie with string to form a bag. Place bag in slow cooker.

2 Cover and cook on low for 1 hour. Discard the spice bag; continue to cook 1-2 hours or until heated through.

YIELD: 3 SERVINGS.

ravioli casserole

Mary Ann Rothert, Austin, Texas

The whole family will love this yummy main dish that tastes like lasagna without all the fuss. Time-saving ingredients like spaghetti sauce and frozen ravioli make it a cinch to make. Children can help you assemble this one.

1   jar (28 ounces) spaghetti sauce
1   package (25 ounces) frozen cheese ravioli, cooked and drained
2   cups (16 ounces) 4% cottage cheese
4   cups (16 ounces) shredded mozzarella cheese
1/4 cup grated Parmesan cheese

1 Spread 1/2 cup of spaghetti sauce in an ungreased 13-in. x 9-in. baking dish. Layer with half of the ravioli, 1-1/4 cups of sauce, 1 cup cottage cheese and 2 cups mozzarella cheese. Repeat layers. Sprinkle with Parmesan cheese.

2 Bake, uncovered, at 350° for 30-40 minutes or until bubbly. Let stand for 5-10 minutes before serving.

YIELD: 6-8 SERVINGS.

chocolate-dipped waffles

(pictured at left)

Taste of Home Test Kitchen

It's so simple to dip waffle wedges in chocolate and garnish them with sprinkles. Kids of all ages will love making and eating these.

1/2 cup semisweet chocolate chips
1/4 cup butterscotch chips
1/2 teaspoon shortening
 4 frozen round waffles, crisply toasted
Colored sprinkles

1 In a microwave, melt chips and shortening; stir until smooth. Cut each waffle into 4 wedges. Dip point of each into chocolate, covering about 1/2 in. on one side; allow excess to drip off.

2 Place on waxed paper-lined baking sheets and garnish with sprinkles. Refrigerate until set.

YIELD: 16 PIECES.

sand art brownie mix

Claudia Temple, Sutton, West Virginia

It's fun to make and give these jars as gifts to friends or teachers. But be prepared—you'll want to munch on some brownies as you make the jars of pretty mix!

 1 cup plus 2 tablespoons all-purpose flour
1/2 teaspoon salt
2/3 cup packed brown sugar
2/3 cup sugar
1/3 cup baking cocoa
1/2 cup semisweet chocolate chips
1/2 cup vanilla *or* white chips
1/2 cup chopped pecans
ADDITIONAL INGREDIENTS:
 3 eggs
2/3 cup canola oil
 1 teaspoon vanilla extract

1 In a small bowl, combine flour and salt. In a 1-qt. glass container, layer the flour mixture, brown sugar, sugar, cocoa, chips and pecans.

2 Cover and store in a cool dry place for up to 6 months.

YIELD: 1 BATCH (ABOUT 4 CUPS TOTAL).

TO PREPARE BROWNIES: In a large bowl, whisk the eggs, oil and vanilla. Add brownie mix; stir until blended. Spread into a greased 9-in. square baking pan. Bake at 350° for 25-30 minutes or until a toothpick inserted near the center comes out clean (do not overbake). Cool on a wire rack.

easy stuffed shells

Dolores Betchner, Cudahy, Wisconsin

I put this recipe together one day when we had unexpected guests. It was an immediate hit and is now a family favorite. Get the kids involved when putting together this simple, savory dish.

- 1 package (12 ounces) jumbo pasta shells
- 1 jar (26 ounces) spaghetti sauce
- 36 frozen fully cooked Italian meatballs (1/2 ounce each), thawed
- 2 cups (8 ounces) shredded part-skim mozzarella cheese

1 Cook pasta according to package directions; drain and rinse in cold water. Place 1/2 cup sauce in a greased 13-in. x 9-in. baking dish. Place a meatball in each shell; transfer to prepared dish. Top with remaining sauce and sprinkle with cheese.

2 Cover and bake at 350° for 35 minutes. Uncover; bake 5-10 minutes longer or until bubbly and cheese is melted.

YIELD: 12 SERVINGS.

spooky hawaiian pizza

Taste of Home Test Kitchen

Pizza is always a hit, and it's even better with a homemade touch. Use your artistry to give popular Hawaiian pizza a silly Halloween personality.

- 1 loaf (1 pound) frozen bread dough, thawed
- 1 cup pizza sauce
- 1 cup (4 ounces) shredded part-skim mozzarella cheese
- 4 slices Canadian bacon
- 3 slices pineapple
- 1 pitted ripe olive, cut in half lengthwise

1 Roll dough into a 15-in. circle. Transfer to an ungreased 14-in. pizza pan, building up edges slightly. Bake at 425° for 10-12 minutes or until lightly browned.

2 Spread with sauce; sprinkle with cheese. Bake for 5 minutes. Cut each Canadian bacon slice into 1/4-in. strips; arrange on pizza for hair. Bake for 5-6 minutes or until cheese is browned.

3 For eyes, arrange two slices pineapple and olive halves on pizza. Cut remaining pineapple slice in half. From one half, cut three thin pieces. Add the half slice and pieces of pineapple for mouth and teeth. (Save remaining pineapple for another use.)

YIELD: 8 SERVINGS.

berry blue ice pops

(pictured at left)

Darlene Brenden, Salem, Oregon

Kids just love these cool and refreshing treats on steamy summer days. It's exciting to come up with new flavors.

- 1 cup sugar
- 1 package (3 ounces) berry blue gelatin
- 1 package (.13 ounce) unsweetened berry blue soft drink mix
- 2 cups boiling water
- 2 cups cold water
- 10 disposable plastic cups (5 ounces)
- Heavy-duty aluminum foil
- 10 Popsicle sticks

1 In a large bowl, combine the sugar, gelatin and drink mix in boiling water until dissolved. Add cold water. Pour into cups. Cover each cup with foil; insert sticks through foil (foil will hold sticks upright).

2 Place in a 13-in. x 9-in. pan; freeze. To serve, remove foil and plastic cups.

YIELD: 10 SERVINGS.

CHERRY ICE POPS: Substitute cherry gelatin and soft drink mix.

italian quesadillas

Annalee Wadsworth, Fallon, Nevada

These little "taco pizzas" are ready in the blink of an eye. You and your child can make as many as you need for family and friends; just assemble, microwave and enjoy.

- 1 package (3-1/2 ounces) sliced pepperoni
- 6 flour tortillas (6 inches)
- 1-1/2 cups (6 ounces) shredded Colby-Monterey Jack *or* mozzarella cheese
- Shredded lettuce and picante sauce

1 Divide pepperoni among the tortillas; sprinkle with cheese. Place one tortilla at a time on a microwave-safe plate. Microwave, uncovered, at 50% power for 30-40 seconds or until cheese is melted. Top with lettuce and picante sauce; fold in half.

YIELD: 3-6 SERVINGS.

EDITOR'S NOTE: This recipe was tested in a 1,100-watt microwave.

corn dog twists

Melissa Tatum, Greensboro, North Carolina

Kids will have as much fun making these cute finger foods as they will eating them! Set out bowls of relish, mustard and ketchup for easy dipping.

- 1 tube (11-1/2 ounces) refrigerated corn bread twists
- 8 hot dogs
- 1 tablespoon butter, melted
- 1 tablespoon grated Parmesan cheese

1 Separate corn bread twists; wrap one strip around each hot dog. Place on a lightly greased baking sheet. Brush with butter; sprinkle with cheese.

2 Bake at 375° for 11-13 minutes or until golden brown.

YIELD: 8 SERVINGS.

cheeseburger pockets

(pictured at right)

Pat Chambless, Crowder, Oklahoma

Ground beef is my favorite meat to cook with because it's so versatile and economical. Refrigerated biscuits save the trouble of making dough from scratch.

- 1/2 pound ground beef
- 1 tablespoon chopped onion
- 1/2 teaspoon salt
- 1/8 teaspoon pepper
- 1 tube (12 ounces) refrigerated buttermilk biscuits
- 5 slices process American cheese

1 In a large skillet, cook the beef, onion, salt and pepper over medium heat until meat is no longer pink; drain and cool.

2 Place two biscuits overlapping on a floured surface; roll out into a 5-in. oval. Place a scant 1/4 cup of meat mixture on one side. Fold a cheese slice to fit over meat mixture. Fold dough over filling; press edges with a fork to seal. Repeat with remaining biscuits, meat mixture and cheese.

3 Place on a greased baking sheet. Prick tops with a fork. Bake at 400° for 10 minutes or until golden brown.

YIELD: 5 SERVINGS.

vanilla ice cream in a bag

Erin Hoffman, Canby, Minnesota

Making homemade ice cream can be an activity for the whole family. Kids can shake the bags until the liquid changes to ice cream. Serve it over your favorite cobbler or fruit pie, or enjoy it alone. No one will be able to resist this one!

- 1 cup milk
- 2 tablespoons sugar
- 2 tablespoons evaporated milk
- 1 teaspoon vanilla extract
- 4 cups coarsely crushed ice
- 3/4 cup salt

1 In a small resealable plastic bag, combine the milk, sugar, evaporated milk and vanilla. Press out air and seal. In a large resealable plastic bag, combine the ice and salt; add the sealed small bag.

2 Seal the large bag; place in another large resealable plastic bag and seal. Shake and knead for 5-7 minutes or until cream mixture is thickened. Serve immediately or freeze.

YIELD: 1 CUP.

pretty pea soup

Paula Zsiray, Logan, Utah

This brightly colored, fresh-tasting soup is one of my daughter's favorites. She purees it in the blender in just seconds then zaps a mugful in the microwave.

- 1-1/2 cups frozen peas, thawed
- 1-1/4 cups milk, *divided*
- 1/4 teaspoon salt, optional
- 1/8 teaspoon pepper

1 Place the peas and 1/4 cup milk in a blender; cover and process until pureed. Pour into a large saucepan; add salt if desired, pepper and remaining milk. Cook and stir for 5 minutes or until heated through.

YIELD: 2 SERVINGS.

marshmallow treat pops

(pictured at left)

Linda Dyches, Round Rock, Texas

My son took these to his first bake sale at school and was the star of the class. I wrapped the pops in clear plastic wrap, tied them with decorative ribbons and stuck the sticks into a piece of Styrofoam for an attractive display. Kids can decorate these with holiday-themed sprinkles or even little candies.

- 3 tablespoons butter
- 4 cups miniature marshmallows
- 6 cups crisp rice cereal
- 24 Popsicle sticks
- 9 ounces milk chocolate candy coating, coarsely chopped
- Decorating sprinkles
- 9 ounces white candy coating, coarsely chopped

1 In a large saucepan, combine butter and marshmallows. Cook and stir over low heat until melted and smooth. Place the cereal in a large bowl; add the marshmallow mixture and stir until combined. Shape into 2-in. balls; gently insert a Popsicle stick into the center of each ball.

2 In a microwave, melt milk chocolate candy coating; stir until smooth. Dip half of the treats in chocolate, allow excess to drip off. Decorate with sprinkles. Repeat with the white candy coating and remaining treats and sprinkles. Place on waxed paper until set.

YIELD: 2 DOZEN.

apple pie in a glass

Dorothy Smith, El Dorado, Arkansas

For a cool, sweet treat with the flavor of apple pie, sip on this satisfying milk shake.

- 1/2 cup fat-free milk
- 1 cup low-fat vanilla frozen yogurt
- 1/2 cup apple pie filling
- 1/4 teaspoon ground cinnamon

1 Place all ingredients in a blender; cover and process until smooth. Pour into glasses.

YIELD: 2 SERVINGS.

little s'more tarts

Susan Martin, Chino Hills, California

If you love s'mores, you'll find these tarts irresistible. The rich filling blends chocolate, marshmallows and cream.

- 2 milk chocolate candy bars with almonds (6 ounces *each*), chopped
- 8 large marshmallows
- 1/4 cup milk
- 1 cup heavy whipping cream, whipped
- 8 individual graham cracker tart shells
- Chocolate sprinkles, optional

1 In a microwave-safe bowl, combine the candy bars, marshmallows and milk. Microwave, uncovered, on high for 45 seconds; stir. Heat 15-20 seconds longer or until the marshmallows are melted; stir until blended. Cover and chill for 7 minutes.

2 Fold in half of the whipped cream. Spoon into tart shells; top with the remaining whipped cream. Garnish with chocolate sprinkles if desired. Refrigerate until serving.

YIELD: 8 SERVINGS.

EDITOR'S NOTE: This recipe was tested in a 1,100-watt microwave.

toad in the hole

(pictured at right)

Ruth Lechleiter, Breckenridge, Minnesota

This is one of the first recipes I had my children prepare when they were learning how to cook. My "little ones" are now grown (and have advanced to more difficult recipes!), but this continues to be a traditional standby in my home and theirs.

   1   slice of bread
   1   teaspoon butter
   1   egg
Salt and pepper to taste

1 Cut a 3-in. hole in the middle of the bread and discard. In a small skillet, melt the butter; place the bread in the skillet.

2 Place egg in the hole. Cook for about 2 minutes over medium heat until the bread is lightly browned. Turn and cook the other side until egg yolk is almost set. Season with salt and pepper.

YIELD: 1 SERVING.

bunny in a cup

Flo Burtnett, Gage, Oklahoma

Kids can transform dishes of instant pudding into cute bunnies simply by adding store-bought sweets. This dessert never fails to delight my grandchildren.

   2   cups cold milk
   1   package (3.4 ounces) instant vanilla pudding mix
   2   twists black licorice
 1/4   cup vanilla frosting
Red liquid *or* paste food coloring
   8   cream-filled oval vanilla sandwich cookies
   8   green jelly beans
   4   pink jelly beans

1 In a small bowl, whisk milk and pudding mix for 2 minutes. Let stand for 2 minutes or until soft-set. Pour into four small bowls; cover and refrigerate.

2 Meanwhile, cut licorice widthwise into fourths, then lengthwise into thirds; set aside. Combine frosting and red food coloring; frost tops of cookies to within 1/2-in. of edges.

3 Just before serving, insert oval cookies into pudding for the bunny ears. Add green jelly beans for eyes and a pink jelly bean for nose. Arrange three pieces of licorice on each side of the nose for whiskers.

YIELD: 4 SERVINGS.

sweet 'n' saucy meatballs

Kim Brandt, Lovell, Wyoming

Making homemade meatballs has never been so short and sweet. Your family will be happy to see these on the menu!

   1   egg, beaten
 1/2   cup quick-cooking oats
   1   pound lean ground beef (90% lean)
1-1/2 cups water
1-1/4 cups ketchup
   1   cup sugar

1 In a large bowl, combine egg and oats. Crumble beef over mixture and mix well. Shape into 1-1/2-in. balls.

2 Place in a lightly greased 11-in. x 7-in. baking dish. Combine water, ketchup and sugar; pour over meatballs. Bake, uncovered, at 350° for 40-50 minutes or until meat is no longer pink.

YIELD: 4-6 SERVINGS.

halloween pizza

(pictured at left)

Flo Burtnett, Gage, Oklahoma

I like to perk up Halloween by having the grandkids make these special pizzas. They can really get creative with the toppings.

- 1 frozen cheese pizza (12 inches)
- 1 can (6 ounces) pitted ripe olives, drained and halved
- 1 medium sweet red pepper
- 1 small green pepper

1 Place pizza on a 12-in. pizza pan. Arrange olives in a circle around edge of pizza. Cut a nose, eyes and mouth from red pepper. Cut a stem and eyebrows from green pepper. Make a jack-o'-lantern face on pizza. Bake according to package directions.

YIELD: 6-8 SERVINGS.

hot dog spaghetti rings

Jared Graetz, Andover, Minnesota

This homemade version of a canned favorite is so delightful and easy. Young chefs will enjoy stirring up this recipe with just a little help from an adult or older sibling. Leftovers are great heated and poured into a thermos for a satisfying lunch.

- 1 package (7 ounces) ring macaroni
- 1 can (10-3/4 ounces) condensed tomato soup, undiluted
- 1 can (10-3/4 ounces) condensed cheddar cheese soup, undiluted
- 5 hot dogs, thinly sliced

1 Cook macaroni according to package directions; drain. Place in a 2-qt. microwave-safe dish; stir in the soups and hot dogs. Cover and microwave on high for 3-4 minutes or until heated through.

YIELD: 6 SERVINGS.

EDITOR'S NOTE: This recipe was tested in a 1,100-watt microwave.

flutter-by franks

Lois Lewis, Bartlett, Illinois

With only two ingredients, these fun and adorable franks couldn't be simpler. I came up with the recipe for my daughter's 7th birthday party. The girls were delighted!

- 1 tube (8 ounces) refrigerated crescent rolls
- 4 hot dogs

Ketchup and mustard

1 Unroll crescent dough and separate into eight triangles; cut each triangle in half. Roll each piece into a ball; flatten to 1/2-in. thickness. For wings, place four dough balls in a square shape 2 in. apart on an ungreased baking sheet. Cut each hot dog lengthwise to within 3 in. of the opposite end. Press a hot dog between each set of wings.

2 Bake at 375° for 14-16 minutes or until golden brown. Place drops of ketchup and mustard below cut edge of each hot dog for eyes and mouth.

YIELD: 4 SERVINGS.

cherries in the snow

(pictured at right)

Barb Cooan, Birchwood, Wisconsin

This sweet, no-bake dish is a definite keeper. The recipe has been in our family for over 40 years.

- 1 package (8 ounces) cream cheese, softened
- 1/2 cup sugar
- 1 teaspoon vanilla extract
- 2 cups heavy whipping cream, whipped
- 2 cups miniature marshmallows
- 1 can (21 ounces) cherry pie filling

1 In a large bowl, beat the cream cheese, sugar and vanilla until fluffy. Fold in whipped cream and marshmallows. Cover and refrigerate for at least 30 minutes.

2 Spoon into dessert bowls. Top with pie filling.

YIELD: 7-8 SERVINGS.

BERRY BLUE SKY: Substitute blueberry pie filling for cherry. Try making up fun recipe names and stories to go along with your favorite flavors!

microwave oatmeal bars

Annette Self, Junction City, Ohio

With so few ingredients and lightning-fast prep, this is a recipe kids will be excited to make again and again.

- 2 cups quick-cooking oats
- 1/2 cup packed brown sugar
- 1/2 cup butter, melted
- 1/4 cup corn syrup
- 1 cup (6 ounces) semisweet chocolate chips

1 In a large bowl, combine oats and brown sugar. Stir in butter and corn syrup. Press into a greased 9-in. square microwave-safe dish.

2 Microwave, uncovered, on high for 1-1/2 minutes. Rotate a half turn; microwave 1-1/2 minutes longer. Sprinkle with chocolate chips. Microwave at 30% power for 4-1/2 minutes or until chips are glossy; spread chocolate evenly over top.

3 Refrigerate 15-20 minutes before cutting.

YIELD: 8-10 SERVINGS.

EDITOR'S NOTE: This recipe was tested in a 1,100-watt microwave.

strawberry cream graham crackers

Taste of Home Test Kitchen

Bananas and a creamy strawberry topping turn graham crackers into sweet, satisfying snacks perfect for between meals.

- 1/4 cup chopped fresh strawberries
- 1/4 cup sour cream
- 1 tablespoon chopped walnuts
- 1 teaspoon brown sugar
- 3 whole graham crackers, halved
- 1 small banana, sliced

1 In a small bowl, combine the strawberries, sour cream, walnuts and brown sugar; spread over graham cracker squares. Top with banana slices. Serve immediately.

YIELD: 3 SERVINGS.

taco salad waffles

(pictured at left)

Trisha Kruse, Eagle, Idaho

Here's a fresh twist on the usual Mexican fare. This recipe is perfect for a build-your-own-taco bar.

- 1 pound ground beef
- 1 cup salsa
- 1 can (4 ounces) chopped green chilies
- 1 envelope taco seasoning
- 8 frozen waffles

Shredded cheddar cheese, shredded lettuce, chopped tomatoes, cubed avocado, salsa and sour cream, optional

1 In a large skillet, cook beef over medium heat until no longer pink; drain. Stir in the salsa, chilies and taco seasoning. Bring to a boil. Reduce heat; simmer for 5 minutes.

2 Meanwhile, toast waffles according to package directions. Layer with the cheese, lettuce, tomatoes, avocado, salsa and sour cream if desired. Top with beef mixture.

YIELD: 4 SERVINGS.

pineapple cherry cake

Melissa Defauw, Auburn Hills, Michigan

When our granddaughter visits on weekends, I try to find something fun for her to do. Since packaged ingredients are simply layered in a pan, this is an easy treat that even a young child can fix.

- 1 can (20 ounces) crushed pineapple, undrained
- 1 can (21 ounces) cherry *or* blueberry pie filling
- 1 package (18-1/4 ounces) yellow cake mix
- 3/4 cup butter, melted

1 Evenly spread pineapple in a greased 13-in. x 9-in. baking dish. Carefully spread with pie filling. Sprinkle with dry cake mix. Drizzle with butter.

2 Bake at 350° for 50-60 minutes or until the top is browned.

YIELD: 12-16 SERVINGS.

s'more ice cream pie

Taste of Home Test Kitchen

Our pretty s'more pie will make you glad you're not camping! Boys and girls will adore the hot toasty marshmallows atop rocky road ice cream.

- 2/3 cup graham cracker crumbs
- 2 tablespoons sugar
- 3 tablespoons butter, melted
- 2-1/2 cups rocky road ice cream, softened
- 2/3 cup marshmallow creme
- 3/4 cup miniature marshmallows

1 In a small bowl, combine cracker crumbs and sugar; stir in butter. Press onto the bottom and up the sides of a 7-in. pie plate coated with cooking spray. Bake at 325° for 7-9 minutes or until lightly browned. Cool on a wire rack.

2 Carefully spread ice cream into crust; freeze until firm. Spread marshmallow creme over ice cream. Top with marshmallows; gently press into creme. Cover and freeze for 4 hours or overnight.

3 Just before serving, broil 6 in. from the heat for 1-2 minutes or until marshmallows are golden brown.

YIELD: 4 SERVINGS.

1. In a small shallow bowl, combine frosting and food coloring. Remove paper liners from peanut butter cups.

2. Holding the bottom of a peanut butter cup, dip top of cup in yellow frosting. Position over center hole on the bottom of cookie, forming the hatband and crown. Add a buckle of Chiclets gum. Repeat with remaining cups and cookies.

YIELD: 32 COOKIES.

pilgrim hat cookies

Megan and Mitchell Vogel, Jefferson, Wisconsin

We dreamed up this combination for a yummy treat to take to school before our Thanksgiving break. Everyone loved them!

- 1 cup vanilla frosting
- 7 drops yellow food coloring
- 32 miniature peanut butter cups
- 1 package (11-1/2 ounces) fudge-striped cookies
- 32 pieces orange mini Chiclets gum

teddy bear sandwiches

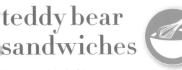

(pictured at left)

Taste of Home Test Kitchen

Cutting a peanut butter sandwich into a cute bear shape gives the classic a fun update. Kids love them.

- 4 slices bread
- 2/3 cup creamy peanut butter
- 2 tablespoons honey
- 1 medium banana, thinly sliced *or* 1/4 cup seedless strawberry jam
- 6 raisins, halved

1 Using a 3-1/2-in. teddy bear cookie cutter, cut out two bear shapes from each slice of bread.

2 In a small bowl, combine peanut butter and honey. Spread over four teddy bear cutouts. Top with banana slices or spread with jam and remaining bear cutouts. Arrange three raisin halves on each for eyes and nose.

YIELD: 4 SANDWICHES.

crustless cheese quiche

Deanna Sheriday, Greentown, Indiana

I've served this yummy quiche for breakfast, brunch and even dinner. Biscuit mix makes it easy.

- 3 eggs
- 1-1/2 cups milk
- 1/2 cup biscuit/baking mix
- 1/2 cup butter, melted
- 1/8 teaspoon pepper
- 6 bacon strips, cooked and crumbled
- 1 cup (4 ounces) shredded cheddar cheese

1 In a small bowl, combine the first five ingredients. Beat on low speed for 3 minutes or until blended. Transfer to a greased 9-in. pie plate. Sprinkle with bacon and cheese; lightly press down into batter.

2 Bake, uncovered, at 350° for 45 minutes or until a knife inserted near the center comes out clean. Let stand for 10 minutes before serving.

YIELD: 6 SERVINGS.

pepperoni rigatoni

Becky Fisk, Ashland City, Tennessee

Children will be proud to put this family-pleasing entree on the table. Parents will love how quickly it comes together and its satisfying taste.

- 1 package (16 ounces) rigatoni *or* large tube pasta
- 1 jar (28 ounces) spaghetti sauce
- 1 package (3-1/2 ounces) sliced pepperoni
- 2 cups (8 ounces) shredded Monterey Jack cheese

1 Cook pasta according to package directions; drain. Add spaghetti sauce and toss to coat. Place half in a greased shallow 3-qt. microwave-safe dish. Top with half of the pepperoni and cheese. Repeat layers.

2 Cover and microwave on high for 5-7 minutes or until heated through and the cheese is melted. Let stand for 5 minutes before serving.

YIELD: 6-8 SERVINGS.

EDITOR'S NOTE: This recipe was tested in a 1,100-watt microwave.

ham and cheese bagels

(pictured at right)

Bev Bronleewe, Lorraine, Kansas

In just 10 minutes, you can whip up a pair of these yummy bagel sandwiches. Pineapple and cream cheese give them a fun twist.

1/4 cup whipped cream cheese
  2 tablespoons honey mustard
  2 whole wheat bagels, split
  1 slice Swiss cheese, halved
  2 slices canned pineapple
  8 thin slices deli smoked ham
  2 lettuce leaves

1 In a small bowl, combine cream cheese and mustard until smooth; spread over cut sides of bagels. On bagel bottoms, layer the cheese, pineapple, ham and lettuce. Replace bagel tops.

YIELD: 2 SERVINGS.

cheddar chicken spaghetti

Ann Robinson, Dauphin Island, Alabama

My son Charlie was a picky eater when he was young, so I put together some of the things he liked. To this day, he says it's his favorite dish! Children will enjoy helping to mix up this family favorite.

  1 package (7 ounces) spaghetti, broken
  2 cups cubed cooked chicken
  2 cups (8 ounces) shredded cheddar cheese, *divided*
  1 can (10-3/4 ounces) condensed cream of chicken soup, undiluted
  1 cup milk
  1 tablespoon diced pimientos, optional
1/4 teaspoon salt
1/4 teaspoon pepper

1 Cook spaghetti according to package directions. Meanwhile, in a large bowl, combine the chicken, 1 cup cheese, soup, milk, pimientos if desired, salt and pepper. Drain spaghetti; add to the chicken mixture and toss to coat.

2 Transfer to a greased 13-in. x 9-in. baking dish. Sprinkle with remaining cheese. Bake, uncovered, at 350° for 20-25 minutes or until casserole is heated through.

YIELD: 6-8 SERVINGS.

chicken egg pie

Judy Bedell, San Miguel, California

My son thought quiche was a funny name and said it should be named "chicken egg pie," which is what we've called it ever since.

  1 tube (8 ounces) refrigerated crescent rolls
  2 cups (8 ounces) shredded cheddar cheese, *divided*
1/2 pound bacon, cooked and crumbled
  1 cup cubed fully cooked ham
  4 eggs
1/3 cup milk
Salt and pepper to taste

1 Unroll crescent dough; separate into triangles. Arrange in a greased 9-in. pie plate, forming a crust; seal seams. Sprinkle with 1 cup cheese, bacon and ham.

2 In a large bowl, whisk the eggs, milk, salt and pepper. Pour over ham. Sprinkle with remaining cheese. Cover edges of crust loosely with foil.

3 Bake at 350° for 20-25 minutes. Remove foil. Bake 20 minutes longer or until a knife inserted near the center comes out clean.

YIELD: 6-8 SERVINGS.

jelly bean bark

(pictured at left)

Mavis Dement, Marcus, Iowa

This candy is as enjoyable to make as it is to eat. The pretty colors make it pop.

- 1 tablespoon melted butter
- 1-1/4 pounds white candy coating, chopped
- 2 cups miniature jelly beans

1 Line a 15-in. x 10-in. x 1-in. pan with foil. Brush with butter; set aside. In a microwave, melt candy coating; stir until smooth.

2 Spread into prepared pan. Sprinkle with jelly beans. Let stand until set before breaking into pieces.

YIELD: 2 POUNDS.

pancake mix in a jar

Diane Musil, Lyons, Illinois

Pancake mix and maple syrup make delightful gifts for teachers, sitters and friends. It's fun to measure these ingredients and put the mix in pretty decorated jars.

- 3 cups all-purpose flour
- 3 tablespoons sugar
- 2 tablespoons baking powder
- 4-1/2 teaspoons ground cinnamon
- 1 teaspoon salt
- **ADDITIONAL INGREDIENTS (for each batch):**
- 1 egg
- 3/4 cup milk
- 3 tablespoons canola oil
- 1/4 cup chopped dried apples *or* cranberries, optional

1 In a large bowl, combine the first five ingredients. Transfer to a 1-qt. jar with a tight-fitting lid. Cover and store in a cool dry place for up to 6 months.

YIELD: 2 BATCHES (3 CUPS TOTAL).

TO PREPARE PANCAKES: Place 1-1/2 cups mix in a large bowl. In another bowl, whisk the egg, milk and oil. Stir in dried fruit if desired. Stir into pancake mix just until moistened. Pour batter by 1/4 cupfuls onto a greased hot griddle. Turn when bubbles form on top; cook until second side is golden brown.

YIELD: 8 PANCAKES PER BATCH.

bunny pear salad

Albertine Sperling, Abbotsford, British Columbia

All dressed up for spring, these darling bunny salads make a cute and festive side dish. What kids wouldn't have a ball making these?

Red lettuce leaves
- 1 can (15-1/4 ounces) pear halves, drained
- 12 dried currants *or* raisins
- 8 whole almonds
- 4 baby carrots
- 4 parsley sprigs

Whipped cream in a can

1 Arrange lettuce on four salad plates; place a pear half cut side down on each plate. For eyes, insert two currants at narrow end of pear; add one currant for nose. For ears, insert almonds upright behind eyes.

2 With a sharp knife, cut a small hole at one end of each carrot; insert a parsley sprig for carrot top. Place under bunny's nose. For tail, spray a small mound of whipped cream at the wide end of each pear.

YIELD: 4 SERVINGS.

cookie pops

Maria Regakis, Somerville, Massachusetts

The kids will have a blast making these delightful chocolate-covered treats. Decorate them like flowers, smiley faces or even rainbows!

1/4   cup creamy peanut butter
20   vanilla wafers
10   Popsicle sticks
4   ounces milk chocolate candy coating, chopped
1   teaspoon shortening
M&M's miniature baking bits, optional

1   Spread peanut butter over the flat side of 10 vanilla wafers, about 1 teaspoon on each. Top each with a Popsicle stick and another vanilla wafer. Place on a waxed paper-lined baking sheet; freeze for 7 minutes.

2   In a microwave, melt candy coating and shortening; stir until smooth. Dip cookie pops into chocolate; allow excess to drip off. Return to baking sheet.

3   Decorate with baking bits if desired. Freeze for 5-6 minutes or until chocolate is set. Store in an airtight container at room temperature.

YIELD: 10 SERVINGS.

santa's coming cookie puzzle

Taste of Home Test Kitchen

This clever confection is easy to make and entirely edible! Whole almonds make it simple for little hands to grasp the puzzle pieces, which are completely removable. Let your imagination take flight with other scenes and stories.

1 tube (18 ounces) refrigerated sugar cookie dough, softened
1/2 cup all-purpose flour
Blanched almonds
2-1/2 cups confectioners' sugar
4 to 5 tablespoons milk
1 teaspoon vanilla extract
Assorted food coloring, decorating gels and sprinkles

1 In a large bowl, combine cookie dough and flour. On a parchment paper-lined surface, roll dough into a 14-in. x 11-in. rectangle. With cookie cutters, cut out puzzle shapes. Slide a baking sheet under the parchment paper and dough. Chill for 5-10 minutes.

2 Remove shapes; place on an ungreased baking sheet. Place an almond on its side into the center of each shape for a handle. Bake shapes at 350° for 7-9 minutes or until edges are golden brown. While still warm, recut shapes with the same cookie cutters to form neat edges. (If cookies cool too quickly, return to oven until softened.) Remove to wire racks; cool.

3 Bake large rectangular puzzle on the parchment paper-lined baking sheet for 12-13 minutes or until edges are golden brown. Immediately recut the shapes inside the puzzle to form neat edges. Cool completely on a wire rack.

4 In a small bowl, combine the confectioners' sugar, milk and vanilla until smooth. Tint frosting with food coloring as desired. Frost puzzle and shapes; decorate with decorating gels and sprinkles as desired. Place puzzle shapes inside puzzle.

YIELD: 1 COOKIE PUZZLE.

pizza for breakfast

(pictured at left)

Joanne St. Angelo, East Providence, Rhode Island

Pizza is popular any time of the day. This breakfast version is so much fun to make and eat. To keep the eggs creamy, be careful not to overcook them.

- 2 eggs
- 1 green onion, chopped
- 2 teaspoons water
- 1 teaspoon butter
- 1 prebaked mini pizza crust
- 1/3 cup shredded cheddar cheese
- 1/4 cup pizza sauce
- 12 slices pepperoni

1 In a small bowl, whisk the eggs, onion and water. In a small skillet, heat butter until hot. Add egg mixture; cook and stir over medium heat until eggs are partially set.

2 Place the crust on an ungreased baking sheet. Sprinkle with about 2 tablespoons cheese and drizzle with about 2 tablespoons pizza sauce. Top with scrambled egg mixture. Drizzle with remaining pizza sauce; sprinkle with remaining cheese. Top with pepperoni.

3 Bake at 400° for 10-12 minutes or until the crust is slightly crisp. Let stand for 5 minutes before serving.

YIELD: 2 SERVINGS.

purple cows

Renee Schwebach, Dumont, Minnesota

Kids will need only three ingredients to whip up this gorgeous treat! Grape juice concentrate makes it irresistible. They will want to make these again and again.

- 1-1/2 cups milk
- 3/4 cup thawed grape juice concentrate
- 2 cups vanilla ice cream

1 In a blender, combine milk and grape juice concentrate. Add ice cream; cover and blend until smooth. Pour into glasses.

YIELD: 4 SERVINGS.

no-bake chocolate cookies

Carol Brandon, Uxbridge, Ontario

This is my son's all-time favorite cookie. He will share just about anything, but these are an exception—he gobbles them up! They travel well in a lunch box, too.

- 2 cups sugar
- 1/2 cup milk
- 1/2 cup butter, cubed
- 3 cups quick-cooking oats
- 1 cup flaked coconut
- 6 tablespoons baking cocoa
- 1/2 teaspoon vanilla extract

1 In a large saucepan, combine the sugar, milk and butter; bring to a boil, stirring constantly. Boil for 2 minutes. Remove from the heat. Stir in the oats, coconut, cocoa and vanilla.

2 Working quickly, drop by rounded tablespoonfuls onto waxed paper. Let stand until set, about 1 hour.

YIELD: 3 DOZEN.

indexes

GENERAL INDEX

Use this index to find the types of recipes you'd like to prepare with ingredients you'd like to use.

ALPHABETICAL INDEX

This index lists every recipe in alphabetical order so you can easily find your favorite ones.